Happy Days
An Autobiography

Happy Days
An Autobiography

by

Lester Biederman

edited by

Nancy Niblack Baxter

1982

Pioneer Study Center Press
Traverse City, Michigan

Reprinted, December 1983

CONTENTS

This book is lovingly dedicated to my wife Anne

PUBLISHER'S PREFACE

Lester M. Biederman, the president of Midwestern Broadcasting Corporation, is a present-day pioneer who has become something of an historical figure in his own time. When radio was in its infancy on the East Coast, he was one of its youngest wireless telegraphers, and he was involved in many interesting phases of its early development, from ham radio to radar.

Coming to the Grand Traverse region in Michigan in 1939, he organized a chain of radio stations and involved himself personally and through the stations in community progress and growth. No other living man, perhaps, has made such a significant contribution to the shape of the Traverse area as it now is, the center of a thriving regional resort and service community for all of northwestern Michigan.

The Pioneer Study Center publishes this autobiography as a part of its ongoing task of interpreting the history of the region, recent as well as pioneer.

INTRODUCTION

The late Dr. Frank Power, Traverse City surgeon and civic leader, worked with Les Biederman on many civic projects from the expansion of Munson Hospital to the bringing home of the Allegheny to Northwestern Michigan College. His 1970 analysis of Biederman's contributions to the area, excerpted from a tape now in the Pioneer Study Center's oral history collection, serve as a fitting introduction to this autobiography.

I first met Les Biederman through my father, who was a native of this area and something of a civic leader himself, although of the quiet sort. One evening shortly after I had come back to town after having been gone for twenty years, my father said, "There is a man I want you to meet. I think you will like him; you two will be good friends. He wants to meet you. His name is Les Biederman."

That evening we went over to the studios of WTCM, which were located in the Anderson Building, opposite the Michigan Theater. My father introduced me to Les, and he was overwhelming even then. He was talking a mile a minute, with all sorts of ideas about what should be done in Traverse City. There was a great big speaker about three and a half feet high in the hallway, and that was blaring away while we talked. We spent about an hour visiting, and from that time on, our friendship evolved.

I first worked with Les in the community when we were trying to expand the hospital and separate it from governmental control to qualify for funding. After the separation had been done, the question came up of raising money for the expansion. Les spoke at a meeting of people interested in Munson's expansion, and he gave a real pep talk. He spoke to everyone about the Mayo Clinic, which had grown into a great hospital in a town more inconsequential than Traverse City. His enthusiasm was the beginning of the growth of a fine medical center here. Les contributed tremendously in fund-raising and committee work, but his real contribution was the enthusiasm and goal-setting he did for us. He set *his* goals high enough to enable us to do what we didn't then have the vision to do by ourselves.

Then there was the college. Some forty years ago the State Legislature authorized the building of a normal college at Traverse City, similar to ones at Kalamazoo, Ypsilanti and Marquette. That college never happened. Old-timers in the town then, always cherished the thought that Traverse City ought to have a school, but they did nothing about it. It wasn't until Les came along that it really happened. Of course, the climate for a college was propitious. Prosperity was here after the war as it hadn't been before, and young people were returning to Traverse City; but it was Les who got the college going.

Out of the college grew the idea of a floating university which Les thought would go around the world, stopping at foreign countries and acting as a floating classroom. I don't know whether that idea is unique with him or not, but it was too much for the town at that time. Out of that idea, though, developed the project to found the Maritime Academy and get the *Allegheny* to use as a training ship. I participated in that project and that trip, which was very interesting.

I'd like to talk about what makes Les Biederman different from other people in Traverse City. When I first returned to Traverse after having been gone all those years and met Les, I was impressed with his dynamic attitude. But what makes him really different, I think, is first of all, a phenomenal memory. He reads very widely and he retains a good deal of what he reads. This gives him an intellectual background for his ideas and activities.

On top of that is his tremendous energy to correct things that need to be corrected. The rest of us are lazy, but Les isn't lazy. We all see stands we should take, letters we should write to radio stations, and so forth, but we don't act. Les sees something that needs to be done, but he doesn't say, "Yes, that's a good idea and somebody should do it." Instead, he says, "That's a great idea and let's do it."

When Les came to Traverse City [1940] people were leaving the town. The young people went away and they didn't come back. There was no industry, and we didn't have good roads.

At one time there had been industry: lumbering, woodworking and potato growing. When potatoes petered out, cherries came in, but when lumbering and hardwood furniture and wood by-product manufacturing went out, when plants like Greilick Furniture Factory, the Basket Factory, and Ovalwood Dish Company closed, there wasn't much left to employ people. The point I am making is that Traverse City was dead on its feet.

What Les brought to the town at that time was leadership, and when he hit the town it was ripe for leadership. There was terrible radio reception here; Les decided he would come to the town and put in a station so people could get good radio reception. That's quite an interesting story. As far as accepting his community leadership when he wanted to get things done, a good many people did accept it. Others, who were accustomed to being the leaders and having an easy role, weren't as sure. Here was Les coming in, saying, "Let's do this and let's do that," and that kind of muddied the waters. Their reaction was only human nature.

Les contributed ideas, and he was an igniter of ideas and people. He supplied the gumption to do something about his ideas. Another thing that interests me about Les is that his interest goes on. Most civic leaders take the path that is pretty well described in Hindu religion, which outlines four phases of life. In phase one a person should get all the pleasure out of life he can, and his hedonistic stage may take one lifetime or it may take several. You have to get all of this out of your system before you can go on to phase two, which is material accomplishment, the gaining of wealth and position. When you get that, and you are satisfied with it, you are ready for the next phase—which is military, community or civic responsibility, recognition, and leadership. Only after you have gone through these three phases are you ready for the contemplative fourth period. In this phase one disavows money, respect, and position, and completely relaxes and finds pleasure in contemplation. They say this takes several lifetimes.

As I reflect on our community leaders here, I believe they are in and out of their responsibility phases. They take the chairmanship of this committee or that committee; and before you know it, at the end of five, or six, or eight years, they quit and let somebody else do it.

Les Biederman, on the other hand, has not done community service as a one-shot deal. His has been an attitude the rest of us do not have; and he thinks differently from the way the rest of us think. With Les community improvement is a twenty-four-hour-a-day, seven-day-a-week business.

He was brought up in what might be called disadvantaged circumstances and I think he is the product of the competition, deprivation, and ambition that result from such a background. Being born with a silver spoon in your mouth is a handicap which he did not have. I observe that many of the leaders in our community have not been born with silver spoons in their mouths, and they have raised themselves by themselves in just one generation. Les is like that; he has raised himself to a position of real success and impact on the community, and that takes very hard work.

Les doesn't bother much with phase one that the Hindus described. He doesn't socialize much. He feels that cocktail parties are a waste of time, and I do too. There is only so much time in a day, and Les seems to spend his on intensive activities. I think he would be happier if he had forty hours a day instead of only twenty-four to do his projects.

Sometimes it is difficult for people to work with Les, because with his restless mind and aggressive personality, he overcomes his fellow workers. He also sees what needs to be done very quickly and is ten steps ahead of others he works with. Practical men cannot always deal with Les's ideas; and boards that have had to work with him have felt admiration, respect, and sometimes frustration in trying to keep up with him. He may work best alone, I think.

Although not all of his ideas, of course, work, he is often quite right about what he feels for the future, for Traverse City and for the country. What he is, is a *visionary*, and I have real affection and respect for him.

CHAPTER ONE

YOUTH IN PHILADELPHIA

I was born August 4, 1911, and I lived my earliest life on a little street known as Weikel Street in Kensington in Philadelphia. When I was four years old, we moved to 2160 Stella Avenue, Kensington, a corner house right alongside a railroad embankment. My father and his family I know literally nothing about. He had married my mother in 1906 and then left her four or five times to go to sea. My father had a problem with alcohol. In fact, that was how he ended up at sea. He was a great ship's cook, and he would go into a bar to meet some people from a ship and they'd get him drinking and off he would go, maybe to Singapore. My mother would have to pawn her rings or anything she had in order to send him money to come home.

After one of these binges, when he "woke up" in Hawaii, he joined the Army. They made him an M.P., and he wore a service revolver. He had thought that the Army would send him back to the States, but they didn't. One day he deserted from the Army. He went first to see his sister, telling her that he had deserted from the Army to see his family. Allegedly this sister had called the Philadelphia Navy Yard and told them that there was a deserter from the Army and gave them the location where he would be, at his home. In the meantime, he had knocked at the door of our home, and my mother appeared, very glad to see him (they were very much in love). I don't believe my mother ever knew he was in this country; she thought he was still at sea. He had left her with a young child, my brother Ed.

Immediately other members of the family gathered around to see him, because he was very much liked by the family. He started to tell his story, with the family gathered around the round oak table; but he didn't get very far. He apparently smelled a rat and went to the front curtain and drew it back to see a U.S. Marine on the front step. He went to the back and peeked out and saw another Marine in back. He announced to the family that he had deserted and that he had caused the family enough trouble, and so he put the pistol he carried to his mouth and pulled the trigger. The bullet ripped through the roof of his mouth and came out his ear and left a hole in the window frame of that house.

He didn't die, but he had blown the whole roof of his mouth out. He spent time in the Halloran Hospital and was given a dishonorable discharge from the Army. After the incident it was difficult for him to get any food in his mouth—they used to have to give him liquid food. He really was quite a cripple until my mother took him to a mechanical dentist who made a rubber plug that would fit in the hole in the top of his mouth. It cost two dollars to have that plug made, and would you believe it, with that plug he could eat, and lead a normal life.

Subsequently, my father stayed with Mother for a while, and I arrived on the scene about three years later. He got a job as an insurance agent with the Metropolitan Life Insurance agency, collecting the debit in our neighborhood for five-and-ten-cent policies. In 1912 and 1913, of course, just before the war, things were pretty rough in Philadelphia; and some people were even calling it a panic. A lot of our neighbors couldn't pay even five or ten cents, and if they didn't pay they would lose their insurance policies. My father would mark some of these people paid who didn't give him the money, and this, of course, caused problems. One day he went to work, and he just never came home.

I was eighteen months old when he left for good. I never knew my father, of course, but I did hear from an uncle some years later that when I was five years old, Father came around the neighborhood. He was inquiring about my mother, and my Uncle Lou Weber took him into a basement and beat the daylights out of him, telling him to keep away from that woman, that he had caused her enough trouble. That was the last word we ever had about my father. As a result of all this, I had no association with my father's side of the family; all my aunts and uncles were my mother's relations. I don't know any of these people on my father's side, never met any of them; as far as I'm concerned, it's a book that has never been opened, and I must admit it is a little strange. Sometimes I am curious.

Growing up in those days in Philadelphia, in what people today would call a poor neighborhood, was a happy experience for me in many ways, particularly since I was always interested in everything that went on around me. I never felt frustrated or supressed, but I just experienced each day as it came to Fishtown. The streets and neighborhood were my play yard, and I remember being in bare feet a lot. Until I was fourteen years old, in the summer I never wore shoes except to go somewhere. No kid I knew ever did. Then when you did put shoes on, your feet hurt.

In Fishtown there were houses with three rooms, one room right on top of the other. Downstairs was a parlor, and a kitchen, which was a shed where the cooking was done. Those big old kitchens had not only a range, and sink, and hot water heater next to that old coal range, but usually a leather couch against the wall also. This was where somebody who was sick could lie down, and it was also the place an extra boarder might go when the scrounge for a place to sleep came at night. Most houses had two bedrooms upstairs, and there was a bath. It seems to me that more people lived in those small houses than live in our houses nowadays. Four or five people slept in one room, and often there was somebody in the parlor too. In those days many people kept boarders. There were immigrants coming over and people would take them in. The Irish would take in Irish, Polish would take in Polish. The only people in my neighborhood who didn't take in boarders were the ones who had eight or ten children.

We were in a poor section of town, and we didn't know it was a poor section. The only thing we knew about it was that one day we would be successful and move out of it and live uptown in a neighborhood of six-room houses. These had a kitchen, dining room, parlor and, to top it off, three bedrooms upstairs—a big deal.

Life was a lot of fun in that Kensington neighborhood. Everyone had an ice box, and the delivery man would come around every morning with a five or ten-cent piece of ice to put in the icebox. One of our favorite icemen was Harry Cossart. My brother worked on his wagon for a while. When Harry would come down the street with that ice wagon, we'd jump up on the step on the back of the ice wagon and grab a piece of ice—our substitute for ice cream on a hot day. We would eagerly wait for Harry Cossart.

There were many hucksters who would come down the street selling produce in proper season. There were the bakers who would come with a basket of rolls, and sweet rolls, and go door to door, and that is how we bought our bread. The milk wagon came the same way. The horses knew the customers and stopped while the milkman knocked on the door to deliver the milk. There was also the soup lady. She would go up the alley with a yoke over her shoulders with two pots of soup. She would alternate one side to the other as she dipped the soup out so both pots would be the same weight. She used to sell pepper pot soup, and she would go down the alley singing, "Peppery pot, peppery pot." You would take this little can or pot out and get some ladled out. This is how this widow made her living. She knew everybody in the neighborhood. The same thing held true for horseradish. A man used to go up and down the street yelling, "horseradish, horseradish." He would grind it right before your eyes, fresh ground; and he would put a little bit on a plate for you so you could use horseradish for seasoning food.

Just about every block had a store—a grocery store, a dairy, a drugstore, or a candy store, maybe several. The grocery stores had tin awnings hanging over their windows, and in the summertime they put out produce—crates of tomatoes, boxes of beans. Oranges were practically unknown, and if you got one in your Christmas stocking, it was a gem. You wouldn't see another one for maybe a year. We never knew what steak was in those days; we lived on soup. There were several different kinds of soup and they were really good.

We got along. Sometimes, when I was a small boy, my mother had to take me to work with her in a stocking factory, putting me in a bin, so I wouldn't get caught up in the machinery. I remember my brother brought prosperity to the family for a while during World War I. He was six years older than I, and he told a shipyard at Bristol, Pennsylvania he was eighteen when he was really fourteen. They hired him, and he became a riveter. Once he was arrested and I cried all night. He was picked up by a railroad detective in the yards picking up coal for the family. The "dick" said he had been throwing the coal out of the cars to get it to the ground.

There weren't many automobiles from 1915-1920 where we lived. A lot of horses were there—when you got coal, a horse-drawn cart would drive up with a chute on it; and a man would turn a crank and raise that load of coal up in the air, so it would come down the chute and into your basement. Every day we'd see a nearby lumberyard's cart driven by a midget and a team of ponies delivering lumber. Streetcars were the public transportation; we had our tricks with them, and one of them was pretty dangerous. We'd take a piece of string tied to a corncob and put it up above the trolley wire.

The wagons would come along on the car tracks; and as the driver would come by, we'd drop the cob on his head and get him mad enough to yell at us and maybe cuss. But there were 650 volts of electricity in those wires, and if there had been any metal in those strings we'd have been electrocuted. We were ignorant, of course. The streets were nine feet wide, two cars not being able to pass; on those old shut-in streets there would be sunlight for only half an hour or an hour a day. It was quite common to see youngsters with crooked legs from rickets. That you never see now.

One of the best things to do was to visit the neighborhood blacksmith shop where they were shoeing horses. Or we'd get coal alongside the railroad, where it had fallen out of the coal cars; or we'd get coke where the engines had spilled their ashes, and we'd use this to heat the house and cook our meals. To get a haircut you simply went to a house up the street; when we were older we'd go to the firehouse and the firemen would put a bowl on our heads and use the horse clippers. We also loved to look at the engines when we were there. They were horse-drawn in those days. We'd go up to Emerald Street to the fire department and get a bowl cut, and we'd all look alike.

If somebody died, nobody had much insurance, so there would be a block party with everybody participating. There'd be a catch-as-catch-can band, somebody playing a mandolin, somebody a horn, always a piano. Then there'd be a dance too, and somebody selling lemonade to pay for burying the person. Everybody had to stick together in order to survive. We had our own kind of fun.

I used to go to the St. John's Sunday School at the Episcopal church on Emerald Street. Behind the church was a large cemetery, and one year there was a big Fourth of July parade. They were drawing a cannon behind horses in this parade. The day before the parade some men had come to the cemetery to paint the little cast-iron markers for Union soldiers, as the men in the parade were veterans of the Civil War—the men from Gettysburg and Shiloh. We didn't know who they were at the time.

And, if a carnival came to town, my Uncle Lou usually took me. He'd throw baseballs and play the other games, and if he won the basket of fruit he'd give it to us because we were the poor relations. Pretty poor at that, to be honest. He'd win dolls, something we didn't want, but he had fun winning them. We boys tried to carry water for the elephants or maybe get a pass to get in the sideshow.

Two of the most wonderful diversions for us all in the Fishtown neighborhood were the Lizzie Boat and the Johnnie Boat, tugboats with wire mesh around the rails so kids wouldn't fall off. They took kids for rides in the summer, picking up from three spots in Philadelphia. The poor kids would get aboard at Allegheny Wharf on Monday at the foot of Bridesburg, and all the kids in my neighborhood would climb on for a ride down the Delaware River. We could watch the big colored man operating the boiler, shovelling the coal, and see the big steam engines operating. Then they'd take us to a place in the Delaware River known as Soupy Island, run by the Campbell's Soup Company, I think. There was a great big tank made out of riveted steel plates, and that was our swimming pool. We'd all go swimming; and then when we were finished, we'd have a lunch consisting of a tin cup of tomato soup and two large soda crackers. Then everybody would load onto the boat and go home after the outing.

The interesting thing was that on Wednesday the boat would go down to another poor neighborhood, Penntreaty Park, to pick up a different bunch of kids. What really happened was that the boats took the same kids—we simply walked six blocks down the river and got aboard in that neighborhood. Same thing on Friday. The crew didn't care—they just wanted everybody to have a good time. I can't find Soupy Island on the map today, but it was somewhere in the Delaware River. I don't know who ran the Lizzie and Johnnie boats—I have always suspected they were connected with the Campbell's Soup

Company because of that tomato soup treat, but I can't confirm that.

On the hot days when we weren't doing that, we were all splashing in the water in a fire hydrant. And on Cedar Street there was a public swimming pool which we used to call the "Swimmo." It was the Cohocsink pool, and it is still there. The way I learned to swim was I was thrown in the pool into deep water and had to swim or drown; that's the way all the kids I knew learned. We used to line up to go in the pool. At the end of forty-five minutes they would blow the whistle, and you would have to get out and another gang would go in to swim. If you had wet trunks, you couldn't get back in. We used to bring another set of dry trunks or go home and get them so we could get in twice, or we would put our trunks between newspapers and lay them in the street to let the traffic run over them until they were squeezed dry. We would also run up and down in the streets drying off, until our trunks were dry enough to pass for a second swim on a hot day.

As I look back now I see the ethnic makeup of those downtown neighborhoods. Some streets were solid Irish, some solid Italian, some Polish or even Lithuanian. This came about because, for instance, some Lithuanian family would be trying to bring relatives over to the Land of Promise and would get them vacant houses. Sometimes before the houses would become vacant these places would be bulging with people waiting to get a place. All the Irish would try to get to be policemen in Philadelphia, all the Italians would try to work for the transit company in street construction crews laying Belgian blocks; they were great stonecutters. The Jewish people would try to become merchants.

There was a nearby neighborhood called "Jewtown." This was over on Williams Street, from Trenton Avenue south towards Port Richmond. There was a block there of all Jewish merchants: a man who made hats, a man that made shoes from scratch out of leather, a family that made candles. They worked together as a clan, and they would bring two or three new people over from Europe each year. It was fascinating to meet these new people. The Jewish merchants would set them up in a business and support them until they made it—they'd all lean on each other. It was great to see people taking care of themselves and each other in those days.

When I was about seven years old we moved to 2146 Monmouth Street in the same neighborhood. When I lived on Monmouth Street, I started school at the Powers Elementary School which is located at Frankford Avenue and Somerset Street. It was an old school when I went there, and it's still in use today. The Powers School was a polyglot of blacks, whites, and immigrants of several countries with heavy foreign accents. One of my schoolmates in the second grade was a huge colored boy who was actually a man, left back four or five times and still trying to learn to read. You didn't get "social promotion" then; you got promoted because you had learned everything in the grade and passed.

World War I had come by this time. The library we used sat in the middle of a city block, a park with a library in the middle of it on Kensington Avenue; and during the War there was a replica of the Statue of Liberty built in that park. There was a platform near the base of this statue where prominent people would come to make speeches about buying war bonds. We kids would listen to the fiery speeches about the war and the Hun and how he was ravaging Belgium. We'd all cheer and wave flags; everybody in the neighborhood would be there, waving those flags. Of course, I didn't know what was going on but I enjoyed the excitement.

About this time, during the early part of the war, my grandmother, who lived with us, decided to make a trip to Toronto to live for a while with my Aunt Rose. I was to go with her. We got on the train and arrived at Niagara Falls, at the border between the U.S. and Canada. First, I need to explain about my grandmother. She was German and had come from Germany on a sailing ship when she was thirteen years old. It had taken her thirty-six days to cross the Atlantic, and it was stormy all the way over. She had told us stories of how she was in steerage, and only once a day was she permitted to come up on deck to get some fresh air; then all the immigrants were shepherded down into the hold again. A lot of the people she was with had run away from home, coming to the U.S. for freedom from East Prussia. At any rate, when Grandmother got excited, she forgot her English and yelled in German. When the immigration man at the border went through the train asking questions, Grandmother started to stumble and reverted back to German. Remember, we were fighting a war with Germany; the offshoot of it was that we ended up locked up in the railroad station as suspicious characters, spies. We were there for two days and they finally sent for my uncle and he came down from Toronto to get us out of the hoosegow. I think one thing that had complicated our situation was that on the train Grandmother had taken out an umbrella and beat the immigration man over the head. She had been very upset, but it didn't do our case much good.

My Aunt Rose lived on a street known as Star Avenue in Toronto, and it wasn't very far from Lake Ontario and its hydro towers. We could hear the wind blowing through the towers, which we thought was electricity humming through them. If you walked a mile, you came to the Canadian National Exhibition Grounds; and there they were training the Canadian Army for the War, in which the Canadians were very active. It was an Army Infantry training ground, and there were guys digging trenches and charging all over. Men in uniforms were all over that place. That was my first introduction to a little piece of the war.

My family was pretty well dedicated to the Henry Diston Saw Works there in Toronto. My Uncle Tone was a top-flight sawmaker there and he made the big band saws that were used in Canada. His son, my cousin Joe, had served his apprenticeship as a sawmaker; and Uncle Tone's son-in-law was also a sawmaker. My aunt and uncle had two girls, fourteen and sixteen, my cousins Laura and Gertrude. When I arrived in Toronto with Grandmother, these two girls grabbed me and gave me the scrubbing of my life. They combed my hair. I had lice, it seemed, as Gertrude later told me.

About six months later my Aunt Annie died in Philadelphia; and my grandmother took me by the hand, and we went back to Philadelphia by train, and from there on I lived in Philadelphia all my life, until I moved to the northwoods of Michigan. Life took on a routine. About this time they were building the big elevated system in Philadelphia, the one which runs from Kensington Avenue to Front Street. It was really a big job with its mammoth steel structure. Right near to us lived a man named Burns, and he drove a wagon while working on the construction project. He hauled the big steel beams from the steel works to the construction site, using a thirteen-horse team to carry each big beam, which weighed many tons. Those horses were three abreast, four groups of three with a lead horse out in front. I remember Mr. Burns sitting up there on his seat, and he would be able to reach out with his whip and tickle the hindend of that lead horse, just as pretty as could be. Once every couple of weeks he would bring that wagon down the street and it would fill that whole street—we kids used to think it was wonderful. He wouldn't let us get up on that flatbed wagon—he was afraid we would get hurt; but when the horses were stopped on the street and he would go into the house to get a cup of coffee or lunch, we would climb up on that seat (which looked like it was five stories tall) and you could look out over those horses.

Many a day we would go up and watch that steel construction work on the elevated taking place. They didn't have cranes in those days; they had steam derricks which had boilers in the back ends, and the man shovelling the coal couldn't even talk to the engineer in the front end; he would have to get out and walk up front to talk to him.

On Sundays during this time my grandmother would meet me after Sunday School and walk me around to see all the relatives—her various daughters. There was Aunt Lou Weber, who lived close to us, and her husband Uncle Lou (two Lous, husband and wife, in one family), and they had five children. Then we would go to visit my Aunt Lizzie, who had fifteen children, ten of whom survived infancy, on Cedar Street.

Cedar Street was an Irish neighborhood; and since nobody had much money in those days, they would go watch the fist fights down on the corner in front of the grocery store. Those Irishmen would knock each other apart, until one of them was knocked flat. Then they'd throw buckets of water on him, thus ending the fight and also that Sunday's entertainment.

From Aunt Lizzie's we'd progress on to visit my Aunt Mame. She was married to Uncle John Schoettler, and they had two sons, Jack and George. Now Uncle John was involved with horses; he sat up with sick horses, and Aunt Mame was the fattest woman you ever saw, except perhaps the Fat Lady in the circus. She was so fat she had to sit in one certain chair, and she had absolutely no lap. She weighed at least 400 pounds. She was a real expert at sewing the covers on baseballs (both hardballs and softballs); she worked like so many people in those days, in her own home. You should have seen her take those two pieces that were stamped out of cloth for the covering, and sew them onto a baseball. Some of the other relatives would wind the filling of balls, measuring the thickness with a gauge. Other relatives worked at the Shoenhut Toy Company, assembling little pianos.

I was about nine years old when my mother and my stepdad, a fireman, got married. They went by streetcar to New York City for their honeymoon. You could, in those days, take a streetcar, going from city to city on one rural interurban after another, until you finally arrived in New York. It took a full day, from early in the morning until late at night to make this ninety-mile trip by streetcar, paying five cents on this car, ten on another. It was a total of sixteen or seventeen streetcar changes.

My stepdad got a new house for us in Feltonville, which is still a part of the city of Philadelphia, and we moved from Kensington with few regrets. Let me give you some idea of what impressed me as a nine-year-old city kid moving into that new suburban neighborhood.

There were trees, there were fields, there were farms. I'd never seen a springhouse before, or a cowyard close up, or a pumpkin in a field. There were rows of houses on Hurley Street, where I lived; but across the street on D Street was a huge farm, the Hessler's. I milked cows now, I shucked corn, I helped the Hessler boy go to the brewery on the wagon and get the feed grain. It's a wonder those cows didn't give milk that tasted like strong beer, or even sauerkraut; since we also fed them from the leftovers from Siler's Sauerkraut Company It was all new and wonderful.

Behind our house was a great big field where horses grazed. On the other side of that field was Green Mount Cemetery. I never got comfortable walking through that cemetery if it wasn't broad daylight. South of our house fields ran down to Frankford Creek, which was really a swampy, mucky swail with muskrats abounding, and willows drooping over it. You wouldn't dare get in that water, but we did push trees over it to cross the stream. We'd pick elderberries and wild cherries around there in season, and dandelions from which we would make wine. Just a little bit to the north of our house was the Craigmeyer farm where all of us kids worked, picking apples and cutting the grass and weeding.

One of the biggest thrills I had was on a certain day off that my stepdad had during this time; on that day he took me for a ride on that big elevated that I had watched them build. I didn't know that after the ride up in the air the train plunged into a subway on the city end of the trip, and it thrilled me. I still get a tug at my heart when I see that elevated in Philadelphia and think of watching it being built and riding it for the first time.

Near us was the Landenberger farm where Jesse Landenberger lived, a friend who was about five years older than I. I have painful memories of picking tomatoes on that farm. What a back-breaking job. We also pulled red beets. We'd load them on a drag, like a sleigh, and pull them behind a horse to the farmhouse, where we'd scrub the living daylights out of them. Jesse and I would drive these vegetables to the wharf on Dock Street to be sold wholesale. He'd leave the farm at

3:30 in the morning, stop for me, and we'd drive to the wharf and unload, getting back home about noon.

When we weren't working, we'd enjoy life together in the neighborhood. One of our favorite things to do was to make and eat ice cream. Nearly every family had something to make ice cream in, a thick can set down in a wooden tub. Ice and rock salt were put between tub and can, and we turned the handle for hours and hours. It sure seems like that ice cream tasted better then, than it does today. Maybe it was the work that went into turning that doggoned crank.

When we had pop, it was probably root beer. We made it by putting the ingredients in bottles with porcelain tops on them with washers. You could re-use the bottles; everybody made their own root beer.

My stepdad was a fireman, and I loved to go to the fire station. He had many jobs in the department, but I best remember him as a stoker. In those days they were still using the old steam pumps, nickel-plated boilers. Some of them were drawn with two horses, some with three. His firehouse had space for three engines. When an alarm came in, the men on watch would pull down on a great big lever that would release the doors of the horses' stalls. Those horses knew exactly where to go and get harnessed, and were they ever anxious! The harnesses were hanging on pulleys, and the firemen would go to the horses and release the harness pulley, put the belly straps on, hook up the traces, and the trucks were ready to go.

The fire in the boiler would be ready to go but not burning: straw, kindling, heavier wood and coal all ready to flare up. When they were ready to roar out, they would light a torch made out of rags dipped in kerosene. The water had been kept circulating through the boiler, just short of boiling hot; it didn't quite make steam. It was my dad, the stoker's, job to make the quick disconnect to the valves of the stationery stove boiler, throw the torch on the fire, jump up behind the horses, and off they would go. Even if the fire was two blocks away, they would be making steam in that boiler.

Those trucks were very heavy and cumbersome. I remember one particular fire in the winter, when the truck went careening around a corner and threw my stepdad off. He went sliding across the ice and hit the curb, and to his grave he carried a big scar right under the hairline on his head from that accident.

When I was about ten, another big thing happened in my life. My stepdad bought me a bicycle, a Plymouth, and it expanded my entire world. I was on that bike for as many hours as I could stay awake. At this time Sears, Roebuck were building a large store and mailing center on Roosevelt Boulevard; we could see it from the neighborhood where we lived. We would watch the clock tower on one of the buildings; now I could ride to it and other far-away places. My whole world of perception changed, and by a series of interesting incidents I had my first introduction to radio, and the dominating fascination of my life. Here is how it happened. One day I was riding down Adams Avenue on a hot summer day. I came down the hill lickety-split onto the melting tar of the street, and the bicycle went out from under me. I landed on my knee; and by the time I had walked home, my knee started to swell up. It got so big I couldn't get my pants on, and I suffered—with hot water bottles and other remedies. Our family doctor, Dr. David L. Suiter, visited me. Dr. Suiter has a story in his own right; he was a member of the first graduating class of Temple University Medical School and was a fine doctor. He treated me for my injured knee; and one day, when he visited, he brought with him a coil of wire, an oatmeal box, a condenser, and a crystal with a cat's whisker, so I could make a crystal radio. With this little set, he said, I could pick up the first peeping sounds now going out in our town, with that wonderful new invention, radio. It was the year 1921. He also had brought a sheet of instructions, and I followed them and got it working; I wound the coil and could almost hear the sounds.

Some of the other kids in the neighborhood helped me limp around and put up a little bit of an antenna, which was necessary to get any reception. I heard a lot of wireless, broadcast with spark transmission.

I also listened to WOO, the Wanamaker Department Store Station, the first station to broadcast in Philadelphia. They would broadcast publically a couple of hours a day and then communicate the rest of the time by wireless from their New York store. All of the afternoon stuff was in code, of course, and since I didn't know what they were saying, I decided to get a book and find out. I started to copy the telegraph code and learned it, at ten years of age. I'm grateful to Dr. Suiter for what he did. I've been very fortunate to be in the electronics industry ever since.

I was going to church at the Boulevard United Presbyterian Church, located at the corner of A and Wyoming Avenue. One day a local member of that church had called, taking a church survey to determine who was going to what church, who was unchurched, and so on, and soon, on a Sunday, I found my ears being washed and my hair combed. I had been enrolled in an institution that was to become a very important part of my life.

For one thing, that church had a Boy Scout troop, Troop 44. The Scout master worked for American Telephone and Telegraph Company in the Bourse building in Philadelphia. His name was Paul Stolz, and he was a wonderful man. That troop still means a great deal to me; I keep in touch with a number of my fellow Scouts now, some sixty years later.

Out of that Scouting experience grew my next small step into the broadcasting business. Two years before, as I said, I had learned the telegraph code; and I had managed to turn into some sort of whiz kid at copying code. I had won a signal award at the arena in Philadelphia for wig-wag signalling. I knew the code backwards and forwards and listened to my crystal radio a lot, and to my new radio with a WD-11 tube that I had saved my money for—a set with one tube in it. By this time broadcasting stations were coming on the air all the time. They played mostly phonograph records as a part of their experimental operation up until 1925. One of the stations was

WIP, which was run by Gimbel's Department Store. There were several other stations during this time—WOO, WDAR, and WNAT. All of these, as a matter of fact, were store stations, run by advertising departments. WOO, that's Wanamaker's station, used to have a noon organ concert with their famous organ, the largest one in the U.S., direct from the store. People would tune into the Wanamaker's concert every day.

We, like the rest of the American public who wanted to hear the radio, listened around our round oak table in the kitchen. There were no speakers; you simply put your headphones into a cutglass dish and the glass amplified the sound for everybody to hear, as they sat being strictly quiet.

Anyway, as I was going one day to the Boy Scout meeting near the entrance to the Green Mount Cemetery, I noticed a house in the middle of the block with two great big poles on the middle of the roof. I recognized them as a super sort of antenna with big insulators. One day, after having watched this antenna for some time, I rang the doorbell and asked the people inside why they had such a big antenna on the roof. That was the first time I had ever heard of ham radio. I met the operator in that house, Eddie Eckert, and was fascinated by his equipment. I began to think about ham radio a lot.

Radio wasn't the only thing to interest me. When I was about thirteen, there was a big construction job done in Philadelphia, and I became tremendously curious about it. It was the Benjamin Franklin Bridge, a suspension bridge across the Delaware River. My stepdad did not have much of a formal education, but he was an avid reader; and he had read in the newspaper about the great suspension bridge designer Ralph Modjeski and his marvelous project. Saturdays I used to ride my faithful bike down to watch the construction of the bridge. In those days you could see work on Saturdays; people labored six days a week instead of five.

As I stood about looking at the bridge and asking questions, one day a young engineer took an interest in me and explained a lot of things about the bridge. I did not inquire his name, but I did know he made the bridge sound very interesting; in fact, one time he took me down in the caisson to show me what the sand hogs were doing down there. While we were there, there was a "blowout," that is, a sandhog came popping up from under the edge of the caisson. They got him up in nothing flat, and I had the experience of seeing him rushed into a decompression chamber, with a doctor in attendance, and saw the air released from him so he wouldn't have damage from the bends.

One day, years later, when I was being presented with the Wolverine Frontiersman Award in Lansing from Governor G. Mennen Williams, I met the man who was being co-honored with me with that same award. D.B. Steinman had designed the Mackinac Bridge. As he shook my hand, Steinman looked at me a minute, asked a few questions, and exclaimed, "You're the kid!" D.B. Steinman, the world-famous engineering genius, was my young engineer on the Franklin Bridge so many years ago.

School, of course, was going on during these years; up through sixth grade I was at the Feltonville School. I would walk each day, starting on Hurley Street, and picking up Bill Holton, a friend of mine (his sister Grace had been the victim of a terrible accident, having been literally cut in half by a streetcar). I would meet first one kid, then another, and by the time we got to school, some blocks away, we'd be an army of kids, thirty or forty strong, singing songs, teasing each other, talking about sports. I think kids who ride school buses today miss a lot.

I hung around the neighborhood when I wasn't riding my bike, and the people on Hurley Street were all wonderful friends. There was Mrs. Wilcox, a widow whose husband had worked for the Federal Reserve Bank. Our next door neighbor was Mr. Ast, and Jim Esmond was on down the street. He'd always call to me as I went by saying, "Here comes Les on his steam-heated stilts." Joe Nagy, the mechanic who could fix anything, was a neighborhood institution. Another man had blueprints, and he'd show them to me by the hour, which whetted my interest in drafting.

We played a lot of games, none of the fancy electronic kind, you can bet, and few costing any money at all. One of the best was "peggy." Here's how you do it. Take a broomstick, saw a piece off about six inches long, and put a point on it. Then you take another piece of the broomstick, two feet long this time, and use it to bat the smaller piece into the air, hitting the tapered end first. You could also play this game like baseball, using these peggies as the ball and bat too.

In 1923 Mr. McClay built the first garage I ever saw close-up, and he used to keep cars there. Model T's became popular right about then, and that garage would be filled with them. I used to make many a fifty-cent piece washing those cars, and I immediately used the money to buy radio parts.

Philadelphia had a terrific park system, and our group of kids enjoyed many of the parks. Fairmount Park runs through a good share of the city on both sides of the Schuylkill River; sometimes it is narrow, sometimes wide. Summer cars (streetcar body with no sides, seats going all the way across) used to run through this park.

We'd ride to Shimony, a little lake where you could rent a boat or go swimming. Woodside Park, a little amusement park with hobby-horses and a scenic railway, was also there. Or we'd go out Girard Avenue to Lemon Hill, where we could picnic, and walk down to the River and "Boathouse Row," where the University of Pennsylvania had a whole lot of boathouses, which were used for skull racing by the various school clubs there. We'd see the coxswain on the back of the boat with a megaphone yelling, "row, row, row." Some of these boats had four men, some eight.

In 1876 the Centennial had been held in Fairmount Park, and some of the buildings still remained. The world's biggest Corliss Engine had been on display, but I did not see it, although I would have liked to. The street lights were either kerosene or city gas, and every evening a lamplighter would go along with his torch and a long pipe, and in the morning he would come and turn them off. The electric lights were all arc lights, and the men would go around and trim the carbons to light them. They were all very brilliant, but there were not many of them in Philadelphia. They had them on street corners, because there was no such thing as a traffic light in those days.

Cooke Junior High was where I went to school in the Seventh Grade. It was located at Louden and York Streets. I loved to wander down into the depths of that fine new school—the engineer was Mr. Pritchard, who ran the boiler and the generators, the two machines that produced electricity for the school. I watched the boiler hand-fired, as the boiler-tender hauled the coal from the bin and shovelled it out into the boiler, and I have been interested in power plants and sources ever since.

Mr. Eisenhart was also a favorite of mine, a mechanical drawing teacher. I took some of my blueprints to school, and Mr. Eisenhart showed me what was what. Mr. Garmen, the science teacher, also spent a good deal of time with me. He was a fire department bug—he knew the location of every fire alarm box in Philadelphia, some 3,000 of them. We would test him by naming a number on a certain corner, and he could tell us just where the box was. He once gave us a list of things to bring in to school and then helped us make a fire alarm device. We wound the coil. Mr. Glassman was also an encouraging man; he taught math.

I used to see a fellow student named Bill Kiker in the halls. It's hard to believe that I'd get to know that young man well enough to involve me in business ventures with him that would last a lifetime. He is still a partner of mine.

The school wasn't quite complete when we went to it (the auditorium wasn't finished), but going there did open up mechanical drawing to me, in spite of the fact that all the buildings were not completed. In the metal shop I learned how to run a lathe, use a vise, and in the woodshop I met Mr. Heckler, who later ran his own school—the Isaac Williamson School of Mechanical Trades. It is amazing that these teachers all gave students inspiration; I don't see enough of that today. Part of it has to do with enthusiasm; teachers don't communicate it anymore because they don't feel it themselves.

On the weekends, when I was of junior high age and a little older, my grandmother would take me down to Cape May, New Jersey. There Uncle Lou had a cottage, really a resort shack and a boat. We'd get up about four o'clock in the morning, take a streetcar to the ferry that went to Camden, then for a dollar and a half ride the ferry train to Cape May. Two hours it took, and on Sunday night, coming back, about a third of the men would be drunk even though the Volstead Act was in effect. All day long they would be drinking bootleg booze out in their fishing boats, then how they would enjoy their ride home! They would walk up and down the train aisles, selling their fish and showing them proudly. I loved that ride.

The ferry boats themselves were also impressive. They were double-ended, with a pilot house on both the stern and the bow. When they'd pull up to the pier, they'd disgorge their passengers and then just pull out the other way; and everybody would stream onto the ferry train.

At Cape May my uncle had a large open skiff, and I used to go out with him sometimes when he fished on the weekends. It was an interesting arrangement with that boat—it was kept inside the cottage, which was built up on stilts. The sleeping quarters were over the boat on the second story, but the kitchen was on the first story with the skiff. There was a trap door in the kitchen that opened right into the water, and it was some garbage disposal. You could watch the starfish and other creatures eating up that garbage as fast as we threw it in.

One of the things we used to love to do on a Sunday afternoon involved that trapdoor. We'd catch some clams, leave them open to the sun until they began to get good and "ripe," and then lower them down through the kitchen trapdoor, in a shopping basket clear to the bottom. We'd see crabs come from all directions to gobble up those clams; and when there were three, four, or a dozen crabs, we'd quickly pull the basket up and, using big gloves so they wouldn't nip us, we'd throw them alive into a pot of boiling water. As soon as they'd turn red, we'd take them up and eat them then and there on the kitchen table.

In the meantime, the basket went down to the bottom again; we'd think nothing of catching fifty to one hundred crabs in one day, the most delicious meal you can possibly imagine.

There were many ships to see at Cape May, international sailing schooners and yachts, and we used to watch the crews polishing the brass and cleaning up the decks. We loved also to walk the boardwalk in Cape May. That place had many amusements, including a rolling barrel to walk through. Fine old Victorian homes had been built on the boardwalk, overlooking the sea. In later years a northeasterner came through, wiping out that boardwalk and ruining a lot of those homes.

During those days of prohibition, the rumrunners were busy. We could see their schooners at anchor three miles out. The Coast Guard kept a destroyer there, and a couple of smaller boats to try to catch rumrunners. Those little boats had Liberty airplane engines on them, and they could go like skat when they were being chased. We'd see these things bring the booze in to shore and autocar-trucks haul it away. I don't know why it was so difficult for law enforcement officers to catch these folks; we kids could always watch these unloading sessions, with the trucks speeding off to take the booze to the Capone gang in Chicago. My cousin Fred Case was a gunner's mate on the small Coast Guard cutter; and as they chased the old rumrunners, Fred would fire the cannon at them, but he didn't seem to cause much damage; he knew the rumrunners pretty well. Well, one night in a chase he broke his leg and had to go to the hospital and was replaced on the cutter by a man who seemed a lot more determined to get his prey. The shells were falling pretty close to the rumrunners and they couldn't figure out what had happened; they found out that Fred was in the hospital, and that answered the question. People on the shore didn't worry much about the Volstead Act; they seemed to think it was a big game to bring the rum in from the boats anchored only three miles offshore.

My uncle's fishing boat had a two-cylinder engine. There weren't any starters in those boats, and to start it you would spin the flywheel back against compression and you'd stand there reversing the flywheel, kicking it back, kicking it back, and it would go "pop, pop, pop" and would run. Beautiful engines with lots of brass. He used to go out twelve to fifteen miles to fish. He could navigate at night by looking at the sky—Wildwood, Cape May, he could even see Atlantic City by its lights. He'd always come right up on the old bell buoy at Cold Spring Harbor.

Those were the days when a lot of us youngsters would get into rowboats, and with the folks' permission, row across the Delaware to the Jersey shore. We'd drop the anchor in the reeds, which were just alive with eels. We would string a whole bunch of worms on linen thread and wind it up and put it over the side, and as soon as we'd feel a tug, up the wormball would come with one, maybe two eels, caught by their teeth, which slanted backwards into the thread. We would catch 150 or 200 eels, which we'd give to people who loved to eat them.

Another thing you could do on the Jersey shore was to get a basket of delicious peaches or tomatoes, which seemed to grow bigger and better on those farms across the river. It really took quite a while to row over there—the river was nearly a mile wide at that point, and the current was strong from the tide.

Mr. Hinman, who was the chief engineer of the traction company in Philadelphia, had a home there at Cornwells, Echo Beach, and he designed a pier for the river. Everybody pitched in to build that pier; we had a dance to get money for the steel, then we all got together and put in the concrete foundations at low tide. Mr. Hinman got us a bunch of air tanks from the brake systems of trolley cars that had been junked, and we had the most wonderful float made out of them. We'd go out on our homemade pier, then out on the float, and then dive into the water, that was six feet deep at low tide and about eleven or twelve at high tide. We'd have the time of our life right there.

The community then took on a dance hall project, again all volunteer work. My cousin Jack, for instance, supervised all of the woodwork and concrete work. We used to have a band, also volunteers, and we'd have kazoos and other instruments. We also had a baseball team which played some of the neighborhood teams. My job at those games was to sell the pop; we made an amazing amount of money from those crowds gathered around to watch the baseball games, almost enough money to build the dance hall.

Upriver about a mile was the remains of a World War I shipyard. There were two partially built ships there; they had been abandoned when the war was over—all heavy planking, bent-up. We'd row up and let the tide carry us by, then just look.

There were many interesting people who stand out in my youth there at Echo Beach—a little man with a foreign accent that everybody called Conny was one. He could do anything, dig a well, or do an odd job. He lived in a shack. Then there was Joe Rickart who embroidered things on shirts and had a factory somewhere. He had an old boat called the "Joe Boat." I used to do work on it for him. Once it sank in about twenty feet of water at low tide, and some of us kids took inner tubes and put them under it and towed it to shore where we discovered a plank that had sprung loose. We put it back in order, and then a couple of weeks later we had to take the whole engine apart, but we got it working for Joe again.

Somehow summertimes at Cape May and a good part of my youth passed rather rapidly. This was because I quit school after eighth grade and went to work. Here is how it happened.

CHAPTER TWO

THE CRAMP SHIPYARD

My grandmother, who had grown up, really, in a very different society, couldn't understand why a big boy of fourteen like me wasn't out earning money and learning to do something practical. She didn't see why I was spending so much time in (to her way of thinking) useless lessons at school. Finally, I gave in to my grandmother's pressure; and I asked three cousins who were working at the William Cramp Shipyard whether there was any chance of my getting work there. One told me to go on over to the employment office, and the outcome of the whole thing was that I came out with an office boy's job—six dollars a week.

There were two guards in the building, and they employed bench boys to run errands for these guards at the south entrance to the building. As I would sit on my bench awaiting orders in the office building of that world-famous shipyard, greeting my eyes there was the imposing sight of a model of the ship named *Cyclops*, which had been built in the Cramp yards. The ship was a large collier designed to haul coal from

Norfolk to Cuba. It had been the pride of the yards, and on its maiden voyage, in 1911, it had been loaded, carrying not only the regular crew which would man it, but also the shipyard crew which would brief the regulars on how to run the engines and generally man the ship.

The ship had left Cuba after unloading and headed back to Philadelphia. One day out, it apparently went down; it carried no wireless, and so it was never known what happened to it; but it was never heard from again. Many of the people in the shipyard had relatives or friends lost with the *Cyclops*. Now today the *Cyclops* is used as an example of a ship that mysteriously disappeared in the Bermuda Triangle. All I know is that that model was a serious, even a grim sight everytime I entered that lobby.

I worked as a bench boy for a month and then got a big promotion—to the iron foundry. I got a raise in pay and was earning $7 a week, which was finally upped to $10. Later I found out that during the last days I was working there, that shipyard was going broke. If I had known that the shipyard was going broke because of my $3 a week raise, I sure wouldn't have accepted it.

I really was impressed by the president of the company. Mr. Mull rode on the elevator with me, and I looked up at him with awe—he had been an office boy too, they said, and he had risen to the top. I had high hopes of following in his footsteps. The company employed four or five thousand men, and they turned out complete ships, making the patterns, castings, boilers, engines, hulls, and plates for the outside, and even the instruments and running gear. The only thing they didn't seem to make were the tablecloths for the galley tables and the dishes to set on them.

My new job was to check in all the 900 employees in the foundry, putting an "X" beside each name; then I would compute the payroll in silver and gold, twenty dollar gold pieces, never paper money. I had to go to the bank and get the payroll on the streetcar, and I was carrying thousands of dollars in precious metals. I carried it in very heavy bags handcuffed to my wrists. It seems odd to me that I could ride in a streetcar without any thought, at the time, of mugging or crime, but I did.

I really earned my seven dollars a week. After I checked the workers in, I visited the Pennsylvania Railroad and Reading Freight Stations to get the car numbers that were sending material to the foundry that day. They would have from between four and fifteen railroad cars full of gravel, sand, iron, coke and other materials for the foundry process; and I would start the office procedure to accept them. That yard was something to behold. They could unload a car every two minutes by dumping it upside down, either into engines for plants like ours or into ships.

As I visited the Reading yard one day, I met George Whertley. I heard him talking about an old interest, ham radio. I told him I could copy code at a high rate of speed but had had no chance to put my skill to practice. The next day he appeared with a telegraph key, a buzzer, and a transformer. "Let's see you transmit code," he said. Through his encouragement, I began to get seriously into wireless; and that sure was a happy day, because it meant more to me than words can describe.

Watching a ship being built from the bottom up back in the early Twenties was a really exciting thing. Up in the mold loft, a very large building, the plans of a ship were laid out as the first step. Then they would make wooden patterns to show the angles and the plates of that ship. These molds were then taken down to the plate and angle shop, where tremendous furnaces glowed with red heat. Here steel beams were softened until they were like taffy, and they were pulled out and bent with special tools to get the angle like it was described in the plans. The plates they produced were sent to the punch shop, where they punched a hole in them with a jig; then they would take the plate or angle down to the ship and, presto! It all fit.

To see the riveters working on those ships was something you couldn't believe. One guy would work with a little furnace, turning the crank on it, with a forge heating the rivets. He'd take it out with a pair of tongs and throw it through the air thirty or forty feet. Then the rivet-passer would catch it with a bucket and carry it to where the riveter was working. Two men would rivet these white-hot pieces of metal into the hole; and by the time they finished, the white rivets had turned black.

I was able to see the ship *Yarmouth* built from the laying of the keel to its launching, and I was on deck the day it went out. The *Yarmouth* burned, with great loss of life, although it had four separate fire-fighting systems on board. This happened in the Caribbean some forty years after its launching.

One of the biggest thrills I had in the shipyard was to watch the construction of the *Malola*, the largest passenger ship ever built in this country, built for the American Hawaiian Steamship Company. Captain Williams from that company was right on hand; he had an office in the shipyards. I remember she was Hull #509. One of the things I watched being built was the *Malola's* foghorn. That thing was so big you could crawl up inside the whistle. I lived five miles away, but when they were testing that whistle, I could hear it all the way to my house.

When those ships were launched, it was a great event. Prominent people would come to break a bottle, and tons of heated tallow were put on the ways of the ship to help it slide. Afterwards, people in rowboats would come in to gather up the valuable tallow for resale. There was usually a minor battle, since the shipyard would send out its own people to gather up these bobbing tallow chunks at the same time that the public was trying to slip in and grab up the tallow and haul it away.

In the nine-story office building where I worked, floors five, six, and seven were drafting areas. One floor designed the machinery for ships, and another was known as the hydraulic department; they designed the hydro-generating motors. Another floor was for hull designing, curve development being important for that. One friend of mine, a draftsman with a slight hunchback, spent many minutes explaining to me how the curves were plotted.

Right outside on the grounds was a special lumberyard for shipbuilding use, and it stored some of the rarest woods in the world: *lignum vitae* (which was used for making the wooden bearings of a ship), also teak, and mahogany. Sharp, good smells used to come out of the lumberyard.

The yard also had a Drydock called the Kensington Drydock. Here ships would be hauled out of the water by means of a marine railway that had a cable. Chippers and caulkers, usually old men, ruled the roost here, and many of them had been before the mast in the sailing days of the nineteenth century. They were usually busy chiselling off barnacles in the old way (airhoses and hammers were just then beginning to come into general use for cleaning ship bottoms). I'll never forget one old man I saw one day, watching a tugboat towing an old ship named *Flying Cloud* downriver. He had tears in his eyes, and I asked him why. He said, "The *Flying Cloud* used to be a clipper ship, and I was her sailing master. They have cut off her masts and now she's hauling coal to a power plant." He had sailed around the Horn in her several times, he told me—in the tea trade. He was seventy-five or eighty. These cut-off clippers, with maybe three or four masts left, were still in use in my teenaged years for hauling coal to New Haven or some other New England port.

One of the first ships in the world with a big diesel engine for cross-ocean passage came in for repairs to that Drydock. Her name was the *Californian*. They brought her in, pulled her out to get the sludge and barnacles off, painted her, and tore the thirty-year-old engine apart. They measured every part of her engine to see how much wear had occurred, and I was amazed at how big that engine was—three huge cylinders which travelled only seventy-five or eighty RPM's.

I also visited New York Ship, which was located right across the river from Philadelphia. Two cruisers were put into Drydock there and completely rebuilt into aircraft carriers—the first was the *Saratoga* and then the *Lexington*. They took off the topdecks and changed them and made new steam turbines, because these ships had to go a lot faster than before. I had the privilege of being on those decks when these new aircraft carriers were launched. It was actually very simple; all they did was let the water come into the Drydock and that floated the ships. Then they towed them out of the Drydock.

The shipyard had many subsidiaries to produce all their marine products. At the Cramp Chain Company, all the chains necessary for a ship were made, from the lightweight chain used to hold pipe fittings (and not much bigger than a toilet chain), to battleship anchor chains six inches across.

What I was getting out of seeing all of this was really an education worth at least one college degree. I gained practical knowledge of how a hydroelectric station operates, how drafting is actually done, how conceptual design becomes reality. I even learned a little history. I had access to the old shipyard records, and I was fascinated and poured over them. Everything had been recorded in beautiful script handwriting. Even in my time much we recorded was done by hand, except sometimes I used a small typewriter. Though the relics of the past, quill pens and penmanship sets, sat on the shelf in our office, they were not used; and nearby in an office I could hear Dr. Parson's secretary, a man, typing away like a machine gun. He had won the world championship for speed typing in Underwood's contest, so a new age was definitely underway.

The shipyard had its own rolling mill, also right on the grounds; there they would bring in rolling stock thirty feet long and roll it into shapes they wanted for various angles for building ships. Other parts of this conglomerate on the grounds were I.P. Marris Company, which specialized in hydraulic equipment; American Lorenti Submarine; American Engineering Company, which made steering equipment; and DeLaverne Diesel.

The iron foundry was a world in itself, a world I got to know very well, since I was really most directly connected with it. The foundry made all the cast-iron parts for ships that those subsidiary companies used. I watched core-making, lostwax-molding, flask-molding and pit-molding. The laborers got forty cents an hour, with the highest paid professional core-makers and molders getting ninety cents an hour. They all worked forty-four hour weeks.

The laborers were mostly Irish and some few colored. The Irish were fresh off the boat. John Kilpatrick was the labor foreman and he was a wonderful guy. I used to visit him at home in Kensington on Sundays. The head man at the foundry was George Matlack; he was a socialite in Philadelphia and belonged to the Union League, a high-powered Republican club in the city. Mr. Matlack used to sometimes send me downtown to the Union League to get his special brand of cigars, or sometimes he would call from the Union League and have me bring him something from the office.

There were all sorts of exotic terms and types of materials connected with the foundry operation. Gravel wasn't just gravel it was *backing*. Sand was called *facing* in the foundry; clay wasn't clay, it was *temper*. Iron wire, they bought by the *stone*, using that old English term. They also used something called *monel* metal in the instruments, and we boys would pick up scraps of this stuff and get the engraving shop to put our initials in it. It looked like silver and wouldn't corrode.

We stored everything in the pattern loft—wooden patterns which became castings. Most of them were split into two parts. Of course, I was not surprised at the wonderful processes of metal foundry work. When I went to Cooke Junior High I used to pass a factory that made barber chairs, and I used to stop in with some of the guys; and they very happily let us junior high students watch.

The original patterns for the castings were made in the pattern loft, and its foreman was Mr. Pratt, an old neighbor of mine from Echo Beach. He made me a drawing board and T-Square and helped me with my first rowboat. It was wonderful to see these men making the wooden patterns of engines and other items to be poured—very precise work. They made the core boxes there, the finest woodworkers I ever knew. The patterns were all color-coded, painted in red for one part, yellow for another, and then numbered for the particular ship they would go on.

The core boxes were taken to the core shop where sand cores were made. Coincidence has played an important part in my life, and when I came to work for the shipyard, I found that my unknown grandfather, George Biederman, and an uncle, Fred Biederman had worked as core-makers in this very department. They were long since gone.

There were actually three foundries there—the iron foundry, the semi-steel foundry, and a nonferrous foundry, where they cast brass and bronze. I used to have to take samples, drillings from test bars, to the chemist for analysis. I saw frames for the biggest diesels ever. I saw big cream separators and big water wheels that went to Lake Victoria or Muscel Shoals. Melting those big runners would take two cupolas of iron which would work all day, and I usually made it a point to be there when that happened.

The cupolas stood thirty or forty feet above the floor of the foundry. The smaller one could melt 100 tons of iron, one melt, and the one next to it could melt 150 tons for a four-hour melt. The cupola looked like a smokestack but was lined in firebrick. Elevators hauled up materials—coke, iron, limestone, all by wheelbarrow. Every so many measured minutes the men would throw in the coke or limestone, and when the doors opened up, we'd see a brilliant blue flame flare out. Air was supplied by an air compressor room, with a couple of great big air compressors run by steam, very old. These were uniquely decorated with the heads of lions, for instance, on the cylinder heads. There were yellow lines on a blue background, decorating these odd but effective antiques. What a roar they produced! It hurt my ears.

A man stood on the platform before the cupola with a whole bunch of red clay; he'd tap the cupola and the metal would be melted inside and would be coming out; when it was time to stop the flow, he'd take the red clay and plug the hole to stop the metal from running, until it was time to load another crucible, from five to thirty tons. Some of the castings that were produced this way weighed ten pounds, some 100 tons.

In the semi-steel foundry, I learned, they did it differently. They had arc furnaces and melted by means of electricity. The nonferrous foundry melted in graphite crucibles underground in pits. They did fantastic things there, and I loved to watch it all. The brass foundry, of course, made things for other places as well as just the shipyard. They had some association with Federal Steel in Lester, Pennsylvania, and anything that had to be cast out of steel was made in Lester and sent to the yard. We used to make propellers for the British Navy and made four sets of propellers for the *Queen Mary*, I believe because we could handle larger castings than could be made anywhere in Britain.

We had the largest lathes in the U.S. in our machine shops, the Cramp Machine Shop, and the I.P. Marris Shop. They could make cannons for battleships for the Philadelphia Navy Yard on the lathe, sixteen-inch guns. We had the biggest boring mill, forty-two feet between the pillars on the thing, that I have ever heard of. That lathe was stupendous. At the same time, in another part of the shop not far away, was a man working a tiny jewel lathe, making a part for a steering mechanism. I'd be watching him, and over his shoulder I'd see the big lathe making cannon barrels farther out in the shop.

The storehouse at the foundry was fascinating too. Here workers could draw trowels of different sorts—heart trowels and flat trowels, lifters to remove small bits of sand from the molds, and strange brushes different from anything you've ever seen elsewhere.

Outside and nearby there were piles of pig iron, sorted and ready to use in the foundry process. Rats would scurry about the piles into their comfortable nests, and we used to call them wharf rats. These huge rodents were as big as cats. I recall that one time a colored man was moving some pig iron and uncovered a nest of young rats. The mother rat, really a huge one, dove for him and grabbed him by the throat. We couldn't get him loose and had to carry him to the dispensary, rat and all. They finally had to cut the rat's head off to get her loose from that worker's throat. The man died, and I'm not sure what the complication was that caused his death.

We had a blacksmith in the foundry named Morris Shaff, a real expert. One day I watched him, when he wasn't busy, take scrap metal and melt it down and make some leaves out of it, like leaves of a tree. Then he welded all his little leaves together and made a pretty little tree, just to keep himself busy. I used to talk to a lot of the men there, and I spent some time with a carpenter named Fred Arthur of Maple Shade, New Jersey. I told him about my little rowboat at Cape May, and he had the idea that I could turn it into a little sailboat. He showed me how to whittle out a mast, how to make a centerboard by making a hole in the keel, so I could sail down the Delaware river, which I did and loved.

All the workers chewed tobacco. They spit into a box of sand, and they tried to get me to take up chewing, but I didn't get around to it. I did all kinds of things to amuse myself during lunch hours and such. I would go out and get the babbitt metal from bearings off of scrap machinery that would come into the shipyard for recasting. I saved this metal and made some molds and cast various objects out of it. One day a man gave me a rough casting of a sundial. I had to do a lot of finish work on it—filing and so forth. I took it up the Delaware River to the Boy Scout camp and mounted it on a stump there. I often wonder if my sundial is still there. It was made of bronze, but it seemed pure gold to me.

Sometimes we'd watch the trains. The shipyard had its own railroad, complete with three locomotives, pushing cars along all over the place. These took the place of trucks in moving things. Another interesting thing we loved to watch was a floating crane called the Atlas, about sixty feet square with a big tower in the middle of it, with a beam going across the tower. It could lift 750 tons. To get maximum lift it had a series of tanks which made up its hull, and they would pump one tank dry and the crane would lean over; they would put the chains around it and then shift the water. They could get seventy feet of lift out of that thing. One time there was a submarine sunk outside of the Philadelphia Navy Yard. They towed our Atlas crane down there and picked that sub up out of the water. There were, of course, hundreds of other cranes running on railroad tracks; and it was all great for a curious fourteen-year-old to see. I was busy every minute of the day, including the lunch hour. I visited the Theodore C. Elemer Company and the Edward S. Corner Company, where they sold ship's hardware; and I tried, as I went, to learn everything. I guess I was something of a sponge.

Anchored in the Delaware River were two tremendous yachts with gold figureheads on the front. One was the Curtis Yacht, *Lyndonia*, and the other the J.P. Morgan yacht, *Corsair IV*. When they came into the shipyard to have work done, I was privileged to go aboard. Once Mr. Morgan came to the shipyard, and I watched him go on the ship to have lunch. On trial cruises the shipyard people would always ask two or three office boys to come out with them. When the *Malola* went out, I wanted to go so badly I could taste it; what a deal it would be to go out on the largest passenger ship ever built in the U.S. I didn't get to. I wanted to go on the *Evangeline*, too, but Billy Purvis, one of the other office boys, went instead. He was killed on that trip, so I guess it was lucky I didn't get to go after all.

I followed the career of the *Malola* through later years. It had its name changed to the *Luriline* and served from San Francisco to Hawaii for many years. It still is the ship of my dreams, replaced only recently by a ship I came to know on a slightly different basis.

CHAPTER THREE

EARLY RADIO

I had quit school when I went to work for the shipyard, but my tremendous desire to learn was still with me. I decided to go to night school in Philadelphia in the "Junta" program. It cost a dollar to register; if you attended class seventy percent of the time, you got your dollar back. I always got my dollar back. I went five nights a week, taking different courses like math, trigonometry, machine design, air conditioning, steam engineering—whatever they offered, I took. I had two dedicated teachers who helped the young men like me learn to do machine work in that program.

As a result of some of the things I learned there and my interest in machines, I became a tool-and-die designer, doing a lot of design work at the drawing board, working at the Edward G. Budd Manufacturing Company.

Weekends I devoted to ham radio. After George Whertley got me interested in ham, he had given me an old call book which listed all the call letters of stations all over the East. There was one in Frankford, belonging to a man named Kenneth Hahn; and I decided to go to his house. There I found out a group of hams were gathering to learn about amateur radio. I appeared on the night of a meeting and became kind of a pet. They instructed me to go down and take an exam and get a license, which I did immediately. The area licensing office was just opening up in 1925. The next year I obtained my commercial license. I was some kind of marvel, it seems; being under sixteen, a special letter had to be sent to the Secretary of Commerce to license me as the third officer of a ship as a boy of fifteen. Then I could be involved in ship-to-shore wireless telegraphy. The Secretary wrote back, "If Lester Biederman has passed the exam, grant him a license." It was signed, Herbert Hoover, Secretary of Commerce.

Later, as I was expanding my talks with hams all over the country, I was frequently in contact with a young man with the call letters Washington, D.C. He became a real ham friend. Only later did I find out that those signals came out of the White House, and that my friend was the son of Herbert Hoover, the President, who had signed my first commercial license. It wasn't protocol to ask a ham friend for his name and address; what an interesting coincidence.

My first ham transmitter was a single tube using copper tubing and a couple of condensers and a tube socket, a Hartly circuit. Crystal control was not in general use at that time; it was a marked improvement when it came in. When you wanted to clean up your sound a bit, you needed to use a rectifier, and since rectifier tubes were almost unknown, we used what were known as "slop jars." These were made by taking a quart jar filled with baking soda saturated with water. On one side you would have a strip of aluminum, and on the other a strip of zinc taken out of old dry batteries. Aluminum and zinc were on opposite sides of the jar—each jar for fifty volts. Bob Herd had an 852 type tube with 3,000 volts; his basement was full of slop jars. His rig was putting out 500 watts of power; my little setup was capable of only two or three watts. We used to communicate tremendous distances with these little rigs.

Our phone transmitters in those days were five or six turns of wire put near to the coil of the transmitter. You connected that to a telephone transmitter and it worked, that is, if you had a rectified power supply.

I got my ham station on the air and proudly went over to see George Whertley to tell him the good news. I found out he had died the previous week. He was just a young man, comparatively, victim of some disease that we don't even have today, which I think happened often. People were bilious, or died of measles, or scarlet fever, or rickets, which young people today haven't even heard of.

About this time I started visiting radio stations whenever I could. While I'd been at Cramp Shipyard, I'd met a lady who was a sister of Mr. J.C. Van Horn, who was a kind of famous fellow in some circles in Philadelphia. He operated the Philadelphia School of Wireless Telegraphy, and they used to train operators to go to sea. It was on Pine Street. He taught the wireless code with blackboard demonstrations going into a lot of the technical aspects of telegraphy. One of the interesting things he had was a radio station in a closet, with call letters WPSW for Philadelphia School of Wireless. It was my first actual experience with a station. He had a lot of enthusiasm, and I was beginning to sop up some of it. Somewhere in this period I got enough to carry me through a whole life of broadcasting. I could never get enough of radio, then or now.

Tommie Howlett was a fish and oyster man who had a station on Broad Street. He'd talk to us and play phonograph records, putting a microphone in front of the old victrola's horn. It sounded terrible. He'd read the newspaper right into the mike and that would be the news of the day. We also visited WELK, which later becamd WDAS. WDAR was Lit Brothers Department Store station and became WLIT. WIP was Gimbels' station. Then there was WNAT, Lennis Brothers' Company station, WWAD, Wright Brothers Electrical Contractors, and WIBG, a station out in Elkins Park, which began broadcasting Sunday church services from a local church. The antenna, which I helped them put up, was in the cemetery right behind the church. The organist in that church was a licensed operator, and that is how they got started. People didn't get paid for broadcasting much in those days; they did it because it was a hobby, almost like amateurs all across the board.

One of the people who urged me to get my commercial license was Charlie Miller, who operated W-3VL ham transmitter. He was a darned good technician, and we established a great friendship. He told me if I got my license within a year, he'd get me a good dinner at Bookbinders. (I got the license but never the dinner, as it turned out.) What I qualified for was a Radio Operator's License, Commercial, Second-class, which was a radio telegraph license. Then, within six months, I had my First-class Radio Operator's License.

One of the most interesting of those early stations was on Pier 98, the south wharves, Philadelphia—WNW. It was a ship-to-shore radio station operated by a man by the name of Haig, who worked all alone there because he couldn't afford to hire an operator. He competed with RCA in Tuckerton, New Jersey, talking to ships at sea. RCA provided all the operators for the ships at sea; and of course if the operators had an option, they would send their messages through the RCA alma mater station, instead of Haig's. Haig operated that station twenty-four hours a day. He would sleep on a mattress on the floor in front of the loud speaker. Wireless could go on all night long, but if WNW call letters would come over the speaker, he would be up instantly, wide awake. He would write down the message, communicate with the station, and then in the morning, when it was daylight, he would wake up and see his notes and be bewildered, because he didn't remember any of his late-night transmissions.

I used to fill in once in a while for Mr. Haig, at times when he would go to his home in south Jersey to see his wife and get his laundry done, finally. I had loved the spark transmitter he had there; it was a real thrill to press that key and see that ring of sparks on the rotating spark cap. That was in the earliest days, though; by the time I was filling in, he had one of the early tube transmitters.

Finally, I gave up working in the tool-and-die trade and entered commercial radio. I guess it was inevitable, but it was brought on by a severe eye problem. I had been working so many hours on the drawing board that I had developed a film over my eyes, and I couldn't see. My stepdad took me to the Wills Eye Hospital, and they told me not to go back to the drawing board, because I was ruining my eyes. I stayed home to recover for a while with a bandage around my eyes; and one day I had a visitor, a man I'd never seen before. Mr. Douglas Hibbs came to see me, saying he represented WTEL in Philadelphia. They needed a licensed operator. I still don't know how he heard about me.

I didn't think I wanted a job as a commercial operator, because I could make twice as much money in the job I had been in, but I decided to visit the operation. The equipment looked pretty sick, but I stayed anyway.

WTEL had gotten started when Mr. Hibbs was in partnership with a Nelson Cocker, a real estate and insurance man in the city. Mr. Hibbs had been the radio editor of the *Evening Bulletin* in Philadelphia, and he had the idea that he should broadcast the football games of the Frankford Yellow Jackets. He had someone build a small three or four watt neighborhood station transmitter, installing it in a wooden trunk, and on Saturday afternoons they would go to the games and string up a little antenna between a couple of poles and open up the trunk—they were on the air! Call letters were WFKD for Frankford; and at those football games was the only time they ever operated. Then they changed its call letters to WTEL, and when I got there it had just recently gone on the air as a fixed radio station.

In those days there were no frequencies or control. In fact, I remember one night all the radio stations in Europe shut down so they could listen to American stations to see if they could pick them up. They did receive some of our stations over there. One of them was WIP, a station in Philly. It had raised its power from 500 to 1,000 watts to see if it could be heard overseas. The bird lovers in the area, I remember, were up in arms because they were afraid of the high power antenna's affect on their feathered friends. A bunch of the men in the town went up on the roof during the time they raised the transmission power, and they had noisemakers and shotguns to scare the birds away from the antenna.

I was turning from a suburban hick to a semi-cosmopolitan, through the contacts I made through the station. George Davis was the radio inspector in our area; he taught me a good deal about the mathematics of the electrical engineering profession. He used to come around a lot; he didn't seem to care too much for Mr. Hibbs and the station, and I've got to admit it was pretty threadbare there in the early days. I took George's ideas and used them, and taught myself, too, out of books. When I later came to Traverse City, George Davis was a consulting engineer for my stations; he had established a little business by then. He had been offered the chairmanship of the antenna division of the FCC. He left Philadelphia after the FCC moved him to Washington, D.C. Directional antennas were just then coming into their own, and George thoroughly understood them. After he left the FCC, he went into business for himself, establishing a partnership with a man named Esterley C. Page. Page and Davis was the name of the firm. Page later became Dwight D. Eisenhower's communications officer during the war, travelling with the General from headquarters in London into France and Germany. He then took the radar equipment developed in World War II and used it to bounce radar signals off the moon to measure the precise distance between earth and moon. I got to know him very well during those years.

When he went, Page sold out his interest in the firm to Davis. Then, after the war, Davis sold his interest to Julius Cohen and Ralph Dippel, and now the firm is Cohen and Dippel. They have been our consulting engineers for forty-two years, certainly a long-time association begun when I was a very young engineer in Philadelphia.

I learned from people and I learned from books. I read technical journals a great deal. Sometimes I went up to

Princeton University to witness the developments being worked on by Ken Armstrong, original research on FM. I used to watch his tests and experiments on modulating the frequencies of radio. He built a radio station in the northern part of New Jersey, and I used to monitor it for him in Philadelphia. I also used to visit that pioneering station WOR at Carteret, New Jersey. Charlie Singer, the chief engineer, and I used to be close friends and he taught me a lot. WOR was the first directional-antenna station in the northeastern part of the U.S.; they were very proud of it. They did a fantastic job of maintenance, and I needed to know about that. I was on duty a lot there at WTEL. One night there was a knock at the door and there was an old friend who had been at Cooke Junior High with me. His father had an ice cream parlor, and I had spent many a happy moments in that parlor with a dish of chocolate ice cream before me or maybe a banana split. I was glad to see Howard Walton, and he was interested in the station. Soon he passed the word to his (and my) old junior-high friend, Bill Kiker, and he'd stop in too, bringing a bag of hamburgers with him or maybe some ice cream; and we'd sit and eat and talk about broadcasting. Bill was fascinated with it too. I taught Bill the theory and code of ham radio, and he and I formed a lifelong partnership at that time. When I formed WTCM, he became the technician; and we have been friends and associates for life. Bill just retired not too long ago from the station.

The station where I was working really wasn't very satisfactory. It had only 100 watt power and divided its times with two other stations. It was on the air only one-third of the time. I tried my best to get the management to change the frequency and put up a directional antenna and become a full-time radio station, but I didn't have any luck.

Let's look a bit at what radio was like in those days in the early Thirties. In those times networks were just getting started. There was CBS and NBC with a limited number of stations for each. In a couple of years NBC started the Blue Network, so they could have two outlets in the big cities. In a typical home, radios were beginning to be common. You put your own together on a bread board by buying parts made by Atwater Kent at a radio store. You needed a detector, an amplifier, and on the floor a storage battery so that when your radio wasn't in use you were charging the battery, and a couple of forty-five volt B batteries to supply the B voltage. In those days the typical radio set had five or six tubes. Later, you could get a radio set all in one box, the whole works, but you still had your A and B batteries.

Philco and other companies had a B eliminator, which was a complete power supply sitting on the floor; when you turned it on, your radio started to work. It would take the AC and would have a trickle charge in the battery to light the tubes and a filter and power supply and rectifier that would supply the plate voltage. You didn't have a transistor radio from your local discount house sitting in a well-marked package. I'm telling you there were some fantastic radios at the time that I am talking about. There was a large horn for a speaker, or perhaps a rectangular speaker made out of airplane cloth. There was no even remotely standardized system for receiving—there were all kinds of combinations. When I first got involved, they didn't even have receivers, and I have been privileged to watch the development of radio from the A and B battery stage to what it is today.

The Philco Battery Company, located in Philadelphia, was in on the ground floor of the industry. They had begun getting involved with the A and B eliminators, and then they began building complete radios. They were hiring people for ten cents an hour; and people were gladly taking the jobs, because there was no welfare, no unemployment. It would put a minimum amount of food on the table to work this way in the new radio industry.

While I was working, during those ten years at WTEL, a lot of interesting experiences happened that meant something to my life. Every week we had a talk on the station by Richard R. Wood, who was secretary of the American Friends Peace Committee. I was so fascinated by the talks he gave on international relations that out of curiosity I went and visited the Friends Peace Committee, which is at the headquarters of the Society of Friends down at 3rd and Arch Street in Philadelphia. Here I met his secretary, Mrs. Price, whose husband was an architect. She was a delightful person, too. Something about these people drew me to them; they were very different, very fine. I seemed to want to associate with them.

I began to go to Friends meeting houses, and I ended up at one at Unity and Waln Streets, the Frankford Friends meeting. Would you believe that on the wall at that meeting house was the land grant from William Penn to build the place?

Now this particular Friends meeting house had not been going continuously since that time—in fact, just recently an attorney known as Walter C. Longstreth, who became a real influence on my life, and his wife Emily, had been sent as sort of missionaries to get this society going again, after it became inactive. It became again a very well-known meeting house, and all kinds of prominent people used to stop in periodically for various reasons; for instance, Cardinal Dougherty, who was Senior Cardinal in the Philadelphia area, the head of the Diocese, would come in for discussion groups. Senators and representatives would come to take part in weekday debates held at the house. One of the people I met was Albert C. Edmunds, who wrote several books on the history of religion. One of his books is a hallmark, comparing the Bible to other religious books like the Koran, passage for passage. What an intellect! He used to sit with his hat on all through the services, because he was brought up in the old Quaker tradition; and he was uncomfortable about women sitting on the same side as men.

That meeting house was really a community center. I even got dragged in—to teach a class of high-school dropouts interested in radio and electricity. I used to have a blackboard lecture once a week, and then on the other class day, I'd take the class to visit AT & T in Philadelphia, where all the long distance switchboards were. Another week we would visit a power plant to see how electric power is produced by steam.

Another time we would go to Conowingo to see the big hydroelectric dam, Western Union Telegraph Headquarters, or broadcasting stations I knew about. Over a period of about three years in the meeting house, I taught numerous people and was given some credit for getting them started in an interest in radio. During the war there were several operators who said they had gotten their start in that class. Those kids asked a lot of good questions, and I found out I enjoyed teaching too.

By the way, those Philadelphia meetings were different from those I see now in the Midwest. They were silent meetings, everybody sitting in silence until someone felt the urge to speak. No preaching or hymn singing. Now and then one of the elders would hand me a Bible and ask me to read a passage. I was scared to death, but I did it; and this gave me a little confidence for public speaking, which was what I needed. Then I was asked to become moderator of some of the weekday public meetings, and this, too, built my confidence. This is the way I learned.

One of the people I met with the Quakers was Richard P. Gregg, who wrote a powerful book, *The Power of Non-Violence*. He went all through Ghandi's situation in India and other situations where non-violence accomplished great things.

I have been privileged all through my life to meet wonderful people, and these have contributed, really, have made up, the meaning of my "happy days." The most wonderful one I met during this period; in 1935 I met my wife Anne Royal Ray. This gal has been a very dedicated, a very loyal, and a very faithful wife; and it hasn't always been the easiest thing I expect. I met Anne in a strange way. A large part of my life, before I got involved with the Society of Friends, I had been associated with the Boulevard United Presbyterian Church. As I have said, I had, early in my life, attended St. John's Episcopal Church in the neighborhood in Kensington; and when we moved to Hurley Street I had begun going to the Boulevard United Church. There I was taught by Hugh Raney, whose son was my friend, the son later became a cop and school teacher. Anne and her sister Bernice were involved in this church, although I did not know them for much of this time. There is a Sunday School class there named after Bernice, who was a wonderful person.

If you went to Boulevard Church faithfully, they kept you hopping with a very busy schedule. I would go to church, then Sunday School, then a young people's meeting in the afternoon, then evening church. What dedicated Scotch-Irish people. Jim Watson was a fine Sunday School teacher I had for eight years, a house painter. On his eightieth birthday, he came to visit me in Traverse City to see what had become of his "young man." I hope he was pleased. Another man was Dr. Bucher, a family doctor who taught Sunday School.

And then there were the people who ran the Young People's Group—one of the finest I've ever seen. We had started with perhaps twenty or thirty young people in that group and then Harold Wolliver and his wife came to be in charge. They began pounding the table and living and spreading the Gospel, and that group grew until we had several hundred young people coming. Then Harold Wolliver had a personal tragedy in his life and no longer ran the group, but his outstanding influence lived on.

Well, anyway, one day the Boulevard United Presbyterian Church was having a picnic, and I rode on a bus to go to the picnic. Jim Ray sat next to me, and he kept telling me what a wonderful person his sister was, and then I met her in person at the picnic. What a coincidence, when they moved the radio station I worked for right across the street from where Anne's family lived! We got very well acquainted. She would come over and visit, or I would go over and have Sunday dinner between shifts. I worked seven days a week, but I was off most afternoons. Then we would go to the movies.

We were married in 1936. I was getting $20 a week again (my salary had been reduced from $20 to $14 and then boosted again), and it was at that time we felt we could get married. Anne was working for the American stores as a clerk in the headquarters downtown. We went on an inexpensive honeymoon at Ocean City and stayed in a little resort hotel. They owed the station money, and we could take something off the tab for them for our two-day honeymoon. We rented a little house for $20 a month, a four-room house. A year later we scraped together enough money to buy a little house on B Street, and we lived there for four years until we moved to Traverse City. We papered, we painted, we worked on that little house, and I had my ham radio station in the back room. It was also during that time that I met a lifetime friend, Al Fischer, whose widow we still keep up with.

I'd been roller skating to work or riding my bike, so I was glad when I had an opportunity to buy my first car—for $50. It was a V-8 Ford. What an engine. It ran on motor oil, not gasoline. When we'd drive to WOR, seventy miles from our home, it took three quarts to get us there and three quarts to get us back. It ate oil, but it gave us wings to get out and around.

During the time I worked at WTEL, I had some time free, as I said, in the afternoons, and I would make it a point to go and see things and meet people connected with radio. Before you know it, I had built a transformer, and I began to build transformers for ham operators. About this time in history it was possible to buy transmitting tubes at a reasonable price, and the hams were going up in power. Instead of having ten watt transmitters, they were having 100 watt transmitters, then 1,000 watters. It was hard to get parts, and transformers cost a lot of money; so I wound transformers for the guys for the cost of the materials. I wound transformer after transformer. The last one I built was number 1,001. I still have some of those transformers that I built in those days around the station. Apparently they did a pretty good job. In those days, you know, you could buy magnet wire for fourteen cents a pound. Now it costs $1.60 a pound for new magnet wire.

A new rectifier started to be manufactured, known as the mercury vapor rectifier tube. I built so many power supplies to use with those mercury vapor rectifier tubes, I built them right up to your ying-yang, so to speak. I sure built a lot of them. Broadcasting stations in those days had 500 and 1,000 watt Western Electric transmitters. They had high voltage generators to deliver the D.C., the high voltage for the tubes. I was able to build a power supply that was quiet and efficient. Instead of having this big generator, I built a three-phase rectifier. To do this I had to find out what a Scott-connected transformer system was. A Scott-connected system enables two-phase power to be converted to three-phase power right out of transformers. So, I got to be pretty expert in building Scott-connected, three-phase power supplies; and I built some four of them for different broadcasting stations.

By late 1936 I had just about given up on WTEL. They were just not interested in becoming a full-time radio station, and I was looking for a real opportunity to move ahead in broadcasting. At that time there was a big survey done by the FCC, and a map was prepared showing the location of all radio stations. Looking at it, I observed that there was not a full-time station in northern Michigan. At first I just glanced at the map and survey. Then I found myself going back and back, fascinated by what I saw there. I gathered information on how many people lived in northern Michigan, what a broadcast area might be, and so forth. Finally a plan evolved in my mind. I determined to build five radio stations in northern Michigan based on what I had learned: Traverse City, Gaylord, Cadillac, Alpena, Petoskey; this would cover the area.

I began to talk to people I knew, friends I could rely on who were also involved in broadcasting. The relationships I organized in those days have endured to this day and are one of the real factors in the success of Midwestern Broadcasting Company.

The first person I spoke to was my friend who visited me at the broadcasting station, Howard Walton; then I approached Bill Kiker, my other friend from Cooke Junior High.

Another person who came in on the dream at that time was Drew McClay, a boy younger than I, whose father had paid me the fifty cents a car to wash the Model-T fords in his garage in Feltonville. Drew got interested in radio also at that time, and our paths began to cross; and so I looked to him when I was forming what would be the new company. He became secretary-treasurer in 1939, when we went official. He retired three years ago, having been with us all those years.

Bill Kiker's brother-in-law, Fred Zierle, also became interested and got involved; he died about ten years ago, and his wife controls his interest in the company now. All of these old Philadelphia friends who started the company stayed with me and it; they are all comfortably retired now. Never was a share of stock sold outside, and the same old associations held true and paid off for all of us.

We met, mostly by night, and talked and dreamed. Why couldn't we put together a station in northern Michigan, we old Cooke Jr. High friends from the Philly area? I thought it would take ten years to build the five stations and promised that was the way we would do it. By 1938 I was hard at work to put something definite into action. We involved my brother in the discussions by the end of that year; he had become vice president of Fisher Body Company in Detroit by this time, and he had a lot of experience in business. He had doubts, he said; the area was undeveloped and he didn't have much faith in its potential. Luckily, he was really wrong about that.

By spring I was able to send him a detailed proposal, and I'm going to include this in full because it shows exactly the kind of investigating, projecting, contacting, and just grinding hard work that was necessary to set up a broadcasting station in those days—also the promise of the American Dream the station held and later fulfilled.

4723 B Street
Philadelphia, Penna.
April 10, 1939

Dear Ed

You have heard me talk about Traverse City, Michigan. Well, that city is now my prime thought for the future. You also asked me several years ago to let you know of any good investments that I may see. Well, here is the dope.

I propose to form a corporation to develop the possibilities of the Grand Traverse Region. The future is very bright as far as I can see. Here is the data.

First I propose to establish a 100 watt nighttime and 250 watt daytime station which could be established without too much cost and with not too high a cost in Washington if it would go through. Then, an increase in power could be requested probably one year after the establishment or perhaps two years. The station could get 1,000 watts power without too much of a problem once you are established. If the present setup remains, and there is every reason to believe that it will, in about 3 to 4 years from now a request for 5,000 watts power could be made with a good chance to get it. By that time most of the 5,000 watt stations operating at present will have 50,000 watts and the station that I propose would fall into that class with the rest. First, however, you must get established and do a good job of serving the locality so that the community itself desires a larger station and will pull for you.

The cash necessary to establish a 100-250 watt station is approximately $20,000 with all purchased equipment. This provides about $10,000 for equipment and the balance to guarantee that it will be a going concern. However, the first $10,000 must be scrutinized very closely; in this case, it will be $3,000 due to the fact that I can construct most of the equipment, especially the most expensive. In fact, the transmitter itself without auxiliaries will cost to purchase from $3,600 to $7,500 depending on the make. It will cost me $300 to construct it, and I would have it ready by the time the license is granted.

When considering the establishment of a radio station, there are many things that must be done, and since I saw you at Christmas, I have been working nearly 24 hours per day on plans etc and most of the ground work has been done. I have taken it up with people that should know and they all agree that it will be a very good, going concern. Among these persons consulted is the Secretary of the Mutual Broadcasting System, who by the way is the Chief Engineer of WOR, the main station of the Mutual Network which reaches you via CKLW at Windsor with studios in Detroit. Then comes a business consulting attorney, a Mr. Walter C. Longstreth who handled the legal end of the purchase of our home.

The opinion voiced by him was go ahead it looks good. No one has been able to find any serious objections to the plans as offered.

One other item forgotten about in mentioning the savings possible by my construction of the station is the radiating system, consisting of a 160′ high tower which is just 10′ above the minimum required by the radio commission. I have a structure designed that will perform like the average 225′ structure is actually 160′ high and costs complete with erection and all at $600.00. The minimum structure required by the Federal Communications Commission would cost in that location between $2,400 and $3,800 depending on the make and exact particulars. This is some saving. I have shown the plans to many engineers etc and there are not any objections to it. Even the chief engineers of WOR and WJZ, the two largest stations in the U.S., say it still is adequate.

When I see you, which may be in a few weeks or perhaps months at the latest, we can go into more details as they make themselves more plain.

The actual cost of the establishment and getting into operation will consist of the following items:

Transmitter	$500.00
Frequency Monitor RCA	500.00
Modulation Monitor	300.00
Radiation system (Tower lights, grounds)	600.00
Studio equipment	700.00
Misc Wiring etc	400.00
	3,000.00
Transmitter Bldg (includes one studio)	1,500.00
Costs in Washington, attorneys etc.	2,000.00
Studio Alterations etc	1,500.00
	8,000.00
Cash necessary until operations are profitable	4,000
	12,000 total

The above costs do not include studio furnishings etc because I do not think that it will be necessary to pay for them. I believe that we can get all furniture necessary together with about 3 pianos for the exchange in advertising with several companies. Also,

I believe that we can get some of the items above listed, for instance the heating plant in the transmitter. This can save probably 200 or 300 in the cost of the building.

You see, the actual cost of investigating and hearings etc will total about $2,000 and this is the amount that will be risked by the stockholders. It will not be necessary to put up the balance, I don't believe (must get definite information from the attorney) until and unless the commission grants the license. Even so, it may not be necessary to put in the whole sum immediately and the whole may never be necessary. I honestly think that if the corporation is formed with $20,000 of outstanding stock, that $10,000 is all that will be necessary to put up.

Now as to whether the station will pay or not. No one as yet has seen fit to doubt this assertion. I have investigated many cities and find this the most promising. It is small and fools most people that tend to look into it due to the unimposing first look. The population is only listed at 12,539. This was in 1930. The census bureau now states that the figure when re-checked will probably go over the 14,000 mark. This is very rapid growth.

When considering the establishment of a station, first we must consider how many stations are competing with programs in a given locality. In Detroit, for instance during the day you can receive with good quality about 12 stations, all with different programs. Therefore you must consider that all of the listeners whose radios are in operation at a given time are not all listening to a particular station. First, there are the big four. Namely NBC red, NBC blue, Columbia and Mutual. Then, there are all of the independents all trying to compete for the audience. Here is where you start to think.

In the Grand Traverse Region, there is no station that gives satisfactory service during the day. IN OTHER WORDS EVERY RECEIVER IN OPERATION IS TUNED TO YOUR LOCAL STATION.

Therefore, the size of the town as far as radio stations are concerned is growing. In considering this remember people will listen to poor phonograph records when they cannot hear the symphony concert direct.

The next important thing to consider is—if a station of this size is located in an area where there are many stations such as Michigan in the lower part and all of Pennsylvania, they will not listen to a station with some static in it, when they can hear another station which is clear. In other words in an area where people are accustomed to poor receptions, they will listen to stations that come in weaker, even though they hear some static. A station such as I propose can reach greater distances due to the patience of the listeners. If it reaches a radius of 25 miles with a diameter of 50 miles the listening area would then become 157 square miles. You must also consider that other programs come in still poorer.

I have some figures to show what would happen considering the static factor. You must keep in mind the following:

> The closest station is 104 miles away, with only 100-250 watts
> The next closest station is 110 miles away with 1000-500 watts
> The stations in Chicago are 240 miles away.
> The Detroit stations are 205 miles away.

None of these stations can supply even the most crude service for listeners during the day. At night, you can hear them but reception is still nothing like what you have been accustomed to. A midget radio will not even work in such a locality. It doesn't have the sensitivity to bring in anything but static during the day.

. . . Now for the corporate setup. I have provided for 4 persons so far in the setup. The situation stands as follows. These figures are by no means definite and may be changed with the consent of all.

	Cash	% shares	Risk Capital
H. N. Cocker	$5,000	40	$ 730.00
Les Biederman	2,000	10	308.00
Drew McClay	3,000	15	485.00
Ed Biederman (if desired)	3,000	15	485.00
			$2,008.00

This is only a tentative arrangement. It may seem funny with such a setup, but H.N. Cocker will not work at the station and will receive no pay, but I will manage it, and Drew McClay will get a salary as operator.

No single individual can control the stock with such a setup.

In considering the risk in the establishment, let us say we must spend $2,000 for the construction permit, and it will cost this much whether or not you get it. If we cannot get it the money lost is shown above in the right-hand column.

It must be borne in mind when considering the risk involved by all parties that as soon as the application is placed, I will begin to construct the equipment and if it doesn't go through, we will have about $500 tied up that I can't use. This accounts for the risk ratio.

As to the future. If the station is granted, the stock could be sold for $50,000 to $75,000 within one year in such a location. The amount of earnings would depend on the desires of the board of directors as to their desires to expand. Here is how it might work:

If the station becomes a 1,000 watt station the value would be

	$150 to $300,000
5,000	250 to 300,000
50,000	350 to 600,000

These figures are of course, depending on good management to make the organization a real success. The opportunity is there.

Now, the reason for my optimism is the actual cost of operations vs the opportunity of advertising selling time.

The actual cost of operations for a full year of operating 16 hours a day and 7 days a week will be (250w day and 100 night) not more than $13,500 per year, and in case of lean days, this could be reduced to $10,000. This means that at the prevailing rates for this class of station a total of 350 hours to 400 hours of ads per year must be sold. In other words, one hour per day will make the station pay expenses without any return to stockholders, but 1½ hours per day out of a possible 16 will pay not less than 10%, 6 for dividends and 4 for expansion.

The chief engineer of WOR, who is secretary of the Mutual chain, has spoken to his attorney in Washington who happens to be one of the best in the country, a Mr. Frank D. Scott, who by the way is from up in the northern Michigan region, and he will see me to talk the matter over. Ordinarily a man of his rank would not take such a small case. He only handles cases like WLW, WOR, WJZ, and such, and therefore it is considered a privilege by me to take such a case before this man. It is possible that he will do the job for a very reasonable price, because the chief of WOR wants to see me get this. If we can expand to the 1000 watt point, we can get Mutual programs and have a real station. The possibility is also open for NBC, but you must bear in mind that the line cost to get programs from Detroit is $23,000 per year and a 100-250 watt station could never afford to carry them.

Please let me know your reaction as soon as possible. You can get me on the phone after twelve at any night at home.

There are many other reasons for optimism, but five pages of letter is a lot. You see, I talked to the chief engineer of WOR for two hours and Walter Longstreth my friend the attorney for three hours and didn't cover all of the grounds as yet.

Hoping you are interested, and also hoping that together the group of four of us can work together and make a lot of money in the next five to ten years.

Sincerely,
Les

From Philadelphia, on B Street, and with one trip in late summer to Traverse City, I worked at organizing the future station. There were so many details and I was at the typewriter every spare minute I had. I wrote to Blaw-Knox Radio Tower Company and other steel and tower companies in the nation checking prices further for the 150′ tower we needed. I had Ben Koenig, a contractor I met in Traverse City, remodel an office in the Anderson Building for me; he was awfully helpful working long distance. I wrote International News Service and the *Christian Science Monitor* news service about the mechanics of using their news services. I wrote to Associated Music Publishers in New York to see about their transcription services and the WPA about the recent transcriptions they had done all over the nation. Hearst radio put out programs called "The American Weekly" and "Jungle Jim Bradley," and I was interested in knowing how we might get them.

I asked for prices on recording and reproducing systems, soundproofing equipment, and all that would be needed in the studio we would build. I was in frequent contact with A.L. LaFranier, President of Rennie Oil in Traverse City, and also the mayor at that time. I wanted the mayor to know about the progress of the new station that the town seemed to badly want. I knew we would meet strong opposition from the local newspaper, as was customary when radio stations entered towns of this size in that time, but with the backing of the mayor and others and the town's obvious need, I felt that whatever happened we could handle and outlive.

About this time H.N. Cocker withdrew; there were some switches; finally, we had almost $16,000 in cash. In addition to the work load involved in getting ready to place the application before the Federal Communications Commission, which involved lots of very technical information about power supplies, modulation systems, and so forth, and the actual setting up of the station to operate, I seemed to get myself involved in Traverse City community interests at this time, before I even arrived to live there.

I began to look around the town with the eye of, possibly, a big city boy, and to see its possibilities. It was a great town, with marvelous people, wonderful natural resources, an interesting history—it could go anywhere. I couldn't seem to stop myself, even at that early date, from dreaming dreams for this town. It could be a center for all of northwest Michigan, packed with interesting institutions and services. Maybe it took a few new people like me to provide a little stimulation at this period at the end of the depression. At any rate, I couldn't keep my ideas to myself as would have been proper for the new kid in town.

What really hit me first was that the old site of what had been this town's big lumbermill, now a sleepy little park called Clinch Park, would be a great spot for a town-wide attraction.

Why not a really good museum? I didn't really know who to write to but sent a few letters around to some of the folks I was meeting in Traverse, suggesting the idea of a museum and I ended up writing to Mr. C.H. Foster, theater manager, interested in doing something for Traverse. I told him about what a success the Franklin Institute Museum was in Philadelphia; in fact, I described it to this stranger in great detail from its astronomy department to its railway exhibits, many of which were paid for by private companies. Then I said I hoped to interest him in helping us to establish a museum in what would be my station's new town. I felt like a brash kid, but I took my nerve in hand and wrote,

> Please do not misunderstand me. I am definitely not trying to tell you what to do, just pointing out what was done in Philadelphia with a little organization and cooperation among just a few of the leading citizens. If this were done on even a very small scale in your already attractive city, it would surely aid in getting conventions and vacation visitors to spend money in the establishments of the merchants of Traverse City.

What happened was that Con Foster did build a museum, and it did become a real attraction to citizens and visitors alike, and I was on my way to a lot of "project-making" that would take me through many years in Traverse City and a lot of miles down the road after the station was built.

Frank D. Scott was busily taking the steps necessary in Washington for us to get our license application submitted. I was really glad such a man was on our team, and it was interesting how he agreed to be our lawyer. I had been asked earlier to come to Washington, D.C., and meet with this man named Frank D. Scott. He was a lawyer practising before the Federal Communications Commission. Prior to that time he was a Congressman from Alpena, Michigan; and when he was in Congress, he had written the Communications Act which governed radio. He knew every twist and turn in that act, every loophole; as a result he was the biggest lawyer in Washington practising before the FCC; he had all the biggest stations, WOR and WLW and places like that.

I had been to about three of these people who had been his clients to try to get them to build a station in northern Michigan before I had taken it on myself to build one; the whole thing he wanted to talk to me about was, "Get off my clients' backs. If you want to build a radio station in Traverse City, then go out there and build it, but my clients aren't interested in building one. They will give you help and advice, but that's all." So I asked him then and there to be our attorney in the matter, and he just looked at me. I think, as a Michigan man, he was a bit interested in me, and his secretary, Jane Kennedy, also from Michigan, seemed to be supportive. I think she took a liking to me and maybe she even talked him into it, because he did agree to represent us. So I had gone back to Philadelphia and got those three principles, Bill Kiker, Drew McClay, and Freddy Zierle to work with me and my brother and we incorporated the Midwestern Broadcasting Station. We formally applied for our license in September, 1939.

That application lay before the Federal Communications Commission for a year before any action was taken. After all that work, we could get no word on it. So I got in my car in Philadelphia and drove to see Mr. Frank Scott in Alpena.

"There's a nigger in the woodpile," he told me, then he made me an appointment to see the chairman of the Federal Communications Commission, Mr. James Lawrence Fly. It was an interesting conversation, and he asked me more questions about the actual operation of a small radio station than you can imagine. "How are you going to pay for this thing?" was one of the main ones. In those days you didn't have a little radio station owned independently; they were owned by a seed company, or a newspaper, or a contracting company, or a department store, or someone who had a special interest; and here were a bunch of ordinary guys who had a little bit of money, and they wanted to build a radio station and run it.

I convinced James Lawrence Fly some way that we had enough get-up-and-go to build a radio station and make it succeed, and a couple of weeks later the Federal Communications Commission granted the permit to build WTCM in Traverse City, and that was the beginning of the Paul Bunyan Network.

CHAPTER FOUR

FOUNDING OF THE STATION AND THE WAR

When Bill Kiker and I arrived in Traverse City, Michigan in my car that day, September 1, 1940, we wondered if we were crazy to have thought of establishing a radio station there. You'd have to have seen it then to understand what I'm talking about. What looked like about three main streets had false-front stores crowded against each other, all built around 1890 and hardly updated since. It looked like a Western movie set on one of the most beautiful arms of the Great Lakes that Nature ever made. A shoe store, a couple of drug stores, two movie theaters (one named the Lyric, the other the Tra-Bay), a couple of run-down hotels, and one square-looking building that seemed to be an effort at modernizing the town (a 1930's version of an historic hotel called the Park Place, which stood out as a ten-story sky-skraper and dwarfed all the other buildings in town). That was it.

Traverse City had been a lumber-boom town. It really wasn't even conceived of until the 1850's, when the only roads north from Grand Rapids were Indian trails, for the most part, and people began to come into the Grand Traverse region to cut the lumber. Then Chicago grew after the Civil War, and Traverse City lumber built it up. The town grew and thrived and even built itself two opera houses and several fine old mansions for the lumber barons, between about 1870 and 1910.

Then everything went bust, in 1915 or so, about the time I was just starting to swim at Soupy Island, and the town died on the vine. Everything looked like it had been preserved from an old-time sepia picture—wooden front porches with rocking chairs on them, brick streets, saloons with rickety signs. A lot of the young people had left to go to Detroit or Chicago. Luckily, the cherry industry had come into the area; most of the farmers and townspeople were getting by, but not much was happening.

What I was to discover on coming, though, was that even if these people were having a tough time making it in the small town that lumber had built and then left, they had a priceless commodity that made their town absolutely unique to me from almost the first time I saw it—a marvelous spirit. Cautious but sincerely friendly, decent, honest, generous to each other and their town, Traverse Cityites were some of the finest people I have ever known, and I still think of them this way.

The people in the town got their news from the *Record Eagle*, a family-owned newspaper that had been around in one form or another for a long time. Needless to say, they were less than eager for an upstart radio station to start up. We were wondering what kind of place we had come to spend the rest of our lives. Right away we met the mayor—Dolph LaFranier, president of the Rennie Oil Company. All during the time we had our application on file and even before we had decided to come, Dolph kept calling us on the phone giving encouragement. We would never have been able to finally make it without Dolph. He put us in touch with people, gave us advice about how to make a go of it and was generally a gem.

Everyone was unsure just what we big city people were about. When we went into the hardware store to buy some conduit wire, they looked at us suspiciously and wanted cash on the barrel head. Not a check, cash. They didn't know who we were. Little by little, we began to make enduring and lasting friendships. We'd sit in at the old Traverse Hotel in the coffee shop at 8 A.M. on those twisted wire chairs at the white marble tables left over from the Gay Nineties. There would be Lloyd Neufer, who owned the hotel, and Dolph, the mayor, and Ervil Watson, the printer. I'd get quite a bit of information from those coffee conversations, and it was in this way that I came to know a little of what Traverse City was really like.

It was a strange, new world. We were used to Philadelphia, and here there were eight operating farms, and the net population was only 9,000 people. The population was listed as 12,539, but 3,000 of those people were in a mental hospital. Nobody was believing that we could have a radio station in this burg. They listened to WTMJ in Milwaukee, and the reception was nothing but a bunch of squawks and static. Attached to the police station was a "radio inspector" named Walt McDonald, who used to go around to people's houses looking for power leaks. With the slightest amount of power leakage, you couldn't get WTMJ at all.

At that time there was a Windcharger Corporation that built battery chargers for farms. The REA was building power lines all over, and these were making the Windchargers obsolete, so they couldn't sell many of these things. They used to build a little steel tower to go along with that generator. Wally Watt and Morry Lezinsky in Sioux City, Iowa, got the bright idea that they could use this tower as a radio tower; we bought one for WTCM. It was 300 feet tall and it was one of the first Windcharger towers used for this purpose.

We had rented space on the third floor of the Anderson Hotel and Ben Koenig had fixed up comfortable quarters, third-floor walk-up. We set to work to put the station together with our own hands, buying supplies, wiring, installing equipment.

On November 11, 1940, we were initiated into the violent weather that can sometimes paralyze the Great Lakes area. We had heard it was like the North Pole, and that wasn't far from the truth. That November night a tremendous wind blew. A couple of ships sank out on the lakes, and one of the car ferries at Frankfort was put up high and dry, so you could walk all around it. That night Bill and I were up in our third-floor studio running conduit to wire the building for the microphones. It got cold and snow started coming in right on us inside. Part of the roof had blown off. When we saw what had happened, we shook our heads and shut down.

Right across the street was the Montgomery Ward store. The light was reflecting off the windows, and we could see to our amazement that they were bending in that strong wind. The traffic lights were swinging and a sign careened down the street. Suddenly there was a loud explosion; one of the big bulk windows in Montgomery Ward had blown out, at the corner of Front and Union. The tires in the window rolled out onto the street and began rolling around. Another, then another huge window blew out, and we went to have a cup of coffee and talked about what a place this was.

While all this was going on in Traverse, Anne was back in Philadelphia, awaiting the birth of our first child. A boy was born on December 5, 1940, and naturally I was delighted although I was frustrated that I couldn't be with them. Here we were one month away from putting the station on the air, but I would have given anything to have been with Anne and that wonderful new boy, my firstborn. There is a funny little story connected with all this. My father-in-law called me on the phone with the news and suggested I send a telegram with a list of suggested names for the newborn son. At that time, when you sent a telegram from Traverse City at night, you couldn't use Western Union, as their office was closed. You could send a telegram through the C. & O. radio operator, through Grand Rapids.

It just so happened that the C. & O. operator had an odd name—Voiley Smith was his name. I made a list of the ten names I had chosen, including the name Ross. He took the last name off the list and added Voiley. What a joker.

Anne came to Traverse City on the train as soon as the station was opened, with that little infant. She had quite a trip. We bought a home, eventually, on Front Street, and it was here we raised our boys Ross and Paul, who was born in 1945.

On Tuesday, January 8, at seven A.M. we put the first signal on the air for WTCM. The people in Traverse City were literally stunned to realize they could actually get a radio station—no static, no fade-out, just rich, pure tones.

We couldn't play phonograph records those first weeks. At that time there was a big battle going on for copywrited music between the broadcasters and the American Society of Composers, Authors, and Publishers. We didn't have a copywrite agreement (most stations didn't), and we were negotiating to clear it all up. We subscribed to an electrical transcription service, and they did have awfully good music. According to FCC rules we had to make an announcement saying, "The following is electrically transcribed." We wondered how we were doing that first week, how the town was taking to us.

Then we found out. On Saturday the Chamber of Commerce gave a luncheon for us, and everybody in town came. There must have been 300 people there. Doug Linder was master of ceremonies and they gave us a great welcome, including a lot of ribbing about the music we were playing. There were some very special guests who had come as a part of the gathering, and this is how they got there. As we had been building the radio station, the city of Traverse City was having a knock-down-drag-out fight with the Pennsylvania Railroad. The railroad owned the right of way for the area right where the boulevard is, along the Bay in Traverse City. The city was trying to get the railroad to move those tracks so they could build a much-needed thoroughfare, but the railroad told the city to go to hell. As I talked to Dolph LaFranier about this, I realized I might be of help. I told him I knew the president of the Pennsylvania Railroad; some years before I had installed a real nice radio reception system in the home of Mr. Clement. I got Clement on the phone and asked if he would see me; he said yes. Dolph and his wife and I got into the car. We took a bunch of Traverse City cherries with us and drove to Philadelphia. We saw Mr. Clement and Mr. Dyess, who was executive vice-president and later became president. We got along fine, but he told the mayor he wouldn't move those tracks for anybody in Traverse City. He would, however, give a good hard look at moving them for his friend from Philadelphia.

He made a big speech to us. It was about how amazed he was that young men would start a company in that day of "Roosevelt socialism," as he called it. Mr. Clement thought it was marvelous that some people had that much faith in the country to start a business out in Traverse City; it did his heart good, he said.

When the Chamber of Commerce luncheon was planned, Dolph LaFranier called and asked if someone from the railroad could possibly attend. Would you believe that four special railroad president's cars arrived in Traverse City? They all were parked down on the waterfront—the president of the Grand Rapids and Indiana line, R.D. McKean; Jim Sims of an affiliated railroad; the president of the LeHigh Valley Railroad, and also one other railroad president. They attended and praised us for the new station, and it made us feel pretty good.

About two weeks after we went on the air, we were asked to broadcast a basketball game from the high school. We got permission and were up there ready to go and then found out we had been cancelled by the school board. The newspaper had objected to our coverage; they protested that they always carried a story about the game the next day. We said all right. That night, to our new crop of avid listeners, we broadcast "dead air." Every five minutes we ran the following announcement: "Although permission was granted to broadcast the high-school basketball game, that permission has been rescinded. We regret we cannot bring you the game; stay tuned for the score." It took all of ten minutes before the president of the school board was in our office giving permission to broadcast the game. Bud Hicks was out there and began to broadcast it, the first one we did in Traverse.

There were lots of little difficulties with the newspaper and some other irritating obstacles, but we met them. Somehow we made it.

We had been on the air about a month or two when I had a group of local people come to visit me. One was Chester McKean, the Quaker minister, one was Harry Hibbard, the local funeral director, and one was Bob Burns, an official of the State Hospital. They told a story of a sad occurence, one which they hoped the radio station could help with, for humanitarian reasons. In Texas, they said, a Salvation Army residence had burned down, and a Traverse City boy named Pat Riley had died in that fire. The body of the poor boy was in the care of a Texas undertaker, and he had embalmed it. They wanted to bring the body of this Traverse City boy back to his home town for burial, and they wanted to know if it would be possible for the radio station to raise the money by making public appeals to bring him home. We thought it was a worthwhile cause, and we started broadcasting an appeal at 6:00 in the evening. We had some church choirs come in and sing for Pat. Then money started to come in, and you never saw a community pour its heart out like that little town did for Pat. We had over $11,000 come in on that one night. Traffic on Front Street was jammed up; people would just leave their cars running and run upstairs to give us money. We couldn't keep up with who was giving what; we ended up with four large wastebaskets filled with money. At 8:00 we began to tell people to stop bringing in money, we had more than enough.

Then the phone rang. It was from a lady who owned a beauty shop in Traverse. She said, "You looking for money to bury Pat Riley? If you want to bury him he is easy enough to find. He is downstairs entertaining one of my beauty operators."

"That can't be the same Pat Riley," I said. She assured me it was. We called the State Police and reported it to our two friendly officers, "Sniff" and "Snoop," Andy Boscham and Clarence Bloomquist. They came down to see us and I told them the story. They proceeded to go up to this lady's beauty shop, and lo and behold, there was Pat Riley! There I was, twenty-eight years old, raising money under false pretenses to bury somebody that wasn't dead. I could hear the gates of Leavenworth Prison clanging shut.

Pat and some other fellow had got involved in some sort of a deal in Texas where they had switched identifications. This was the other fellow who had been burned in Texas; Pat had hitchhiked home. For weeks we asked people to come in and get their money, and they did. We still had between four and five thousand dollars left over. We didn't know what to do with it; there it sat in the bank. We didn't know who had brought it in; there were no records. After many months had gone by, and the war came, the town wanted to start a USO. We took the $4,000 and put it in the USO to give it a start.

As luck would have it, years later the wife of Pat Riley came to work for our company and just recently retired.

December 7, 1941. We had been on the air less than one year. One Sunday I received a telephone call from the Associated Press man who said, "Go down to the office and watch your printer." I zipped down to the office and the story started coming in. Pearl Harbor was still under attack from the Japanese, and I went on the air to announce that a United States base had been attacked and all our lives, mine, the people of Traverse City and the radio station itself would be changed.

Things in Traverse City shifted gears almost right away, as I'm sure they did all over the country. Draft Boards were established; people started disappearing from the streets; we started hearing about and talking about military factors. Young men from the town were enlisting in the Air Corps, while boys I knew were enlisting in the Navy. It was a change and a moving experience to go to the railroad station to see these men marching off to war. Some were leaving families, and it was heart-rending to watch, because nobody really knew what was going on. If you remember, in the Pacific the enemy had us on the run.

At the station, of course, we covered a lot of war news, both nationally and locally. We also published a weekly newspaper called *Your Letter From Home*, with local news for our boys, for instance, that the kids pushed over the outhouse in back of Joe Smith's house and things of that nature, things that didn't appear in the city newspaper. A young lady in the office became a kind of model for it, a very attractive young lady, Ginny Halsal, a beautiful blond, and she became the pinup gal for hundreds of boys all over the world. We received over a thousand shoulder pads from boys who sent them to us. Every town had something like this, and it seemed a nice touch from northern Michigan to the boys doing their duty for the country. Ervil Watson used to print it for us, and we received hundreds of letters from APO's and would read them on the air.

In terms of personnel, some people were leaving us and other people were coming to take their places. We had some people working for a short term. These were boys who had enlisted in the Air Corps, and they wouldn't be called for six months, or some people who would be going into specialized Navy training. They couldn't get jobs while they were waiting because an employer was required to give a serviceman a job when he came back, and the people in our town were often afraid they wouldn't be able to give them a job.

We were reckless and we hired a whole bunch of them, and they became very precious to us all. Many returned to Traverse City and became friends of ours to this day.

I received a telephone call from Charlie Singer of WOR one day. He was now with the government, with the Operations Research Department of the Pentagon, part of the Army Signal Corps. He was involved in the development of electronic warfare. What he had to say to me over the phone that day was, "Les, I need you. Come on down to Washington." It wasn't all that easy for me to go to Washington. I had a problem. I was running the station and didn't know who would run it. My associate Bill Kiker had already enlisted, and he was off to the wars. After about five letters and several irate telephone calls from the War Department demanding my presence I finally appeared in Washington and was sworn in, occupying a desk in the Pentagon Building, 3 D-3 20 in the Pentagon.

There were twenty people already in this department and I made twenty-one. A whole new world had opened up all of a sudden—the people that I was working with, the job that I did. It was tremendous. The man who headed up the department was William I. Everett. He was the Dean of Electrical Engineering at Ohio State University, the best-known theoretical engineer in the broadcasting industry. He had hosted an annual meeting at Ohio State each year, where all of us would go and get our wits sharpened up on new developments in the broadcasting world. He had also written a number of books, and it was great to be on his team. Everett's assistant was Dr. Lynn Smeby, a consulting engineer in the electronics profession. Another of the top men was Dr. Fulton Cutting, who was one of the biggest stockholders in the Colonial Radio Company of Rochester, New York. He was the man who invented the radio loud-speaker.

Then there was Carl Smith, a great guy, who headed up the Cleveland Institute of Radio Engineering, a large correspondence school, and Dr. Kenneth Norton, a mathematician who came from the Bureau of Standards. He knew more about antennas, radiation, and reflections in the atmosphere than any other man in this country. Arthur Omberg was also there, and he was a fine engineer, the chief engineer at WSM in Nashville; and there was John Campbell, who worked with me, also from WSM; and Fred Clark, from Rochester, Minnesota, who was chief engineer from KROC, a fine radio station. I learned a great deal from all of these very fine people.

Beyond these were the many "greats" of the radio industry who worked with us—people like W. Watson Watt, who had developed radar, CHL radar, which kept the Messerschmitts at bay in London, making it possible for British pilots to hold them off and also to locate the bombers coming into England. He was a tremendous guy. We made many trips to Camp Evans, New Jersey. These were headed up by Paul Watson, who became Colonel Paul Watson during the war, becoming head of research. He died at his desk; he was a very dedicated man.

There was also General Reader of Ft. Monmouth, New Jersey, involved in electronic development. Then we went to Florida, to Camp Murphy, Hobe Sound, just above Palm Beach. Camp Murphy was the Signal Corps training school where radar technicians were trained. There I made many, many friends from the electronics industry. One of them was John Ryder, who published the Ryder manuals on how to fix radio or television sets.

One of the most interesting people that I met was Captain Bell, who was the man who was in Pearl Harbor when the Japanese bombed. He was operating the first experimental radar station in the Hawaiian Islands, and he reported the Jap planes coming in. Everybody in the Islands thought he must be insane, but he reported the planes coming in some forty minutes before they arrived at Pearl Harbor, having seen them on that earliest radar. At this time in Washington, D.C., we saw radar develop from the very first, crude, experimental device to the fine-honed instrument it is today.

One of the men I worked with became General Eisenhower's electronics consultant. This man was Esterley Page, a partner of Page and Davis that I have referred to earlier. He was a real whiz kid, the guy who bounced the radar signals off the moon after the War, to determine the distance from the earth to the moon and also to some of the other planets. Quite a fellow.

The War was a very busy time, and we spent a lot of it straightening out this hassle, straightening out that hassle, visiting factories, being sure that everyone was doing everything right, as electronic wartime equipment was produced.

Two people I met when I went to Washington were two brothers from T.C., George and Bill Schulgen. Their sisters lived in Traverse City. Bill Schulgen was a full colonel, the chief of air staff for the Asiatic Theater. I got acquainted with him, and every evening I was able to see the map change as troops moved—Merrill's Maurauders moving and that sort of thing. I had an opportunity, far beyond what any normal news person would be able to see, to view what was happening in this theater of the war. His brother, George Schulgen, was an aide to General George Marshall. George Schulgen was also a full colonel; during the early days of the war he was made a brigadier general attached to the Eastern Air Defense Command, and I had the opportunity of having dinner with him and his staff at Bookbinders Restaurant in Philadelphia. He was then made chief of the Intelligence Group of the Twentieth Air Force, headed by Curt LeMay.

On the night before the Twentieth Air Force staff left Washington to go to the South Pacific (remember, they were the ones who had the B-29's, bombing Tokyo and finally getting the job of delivering the Atomic Bomb), there was a party held at Ft. Meyer at George Schulgen's home. General George Marshall, General Krichelow, and General Tom Power stopped in, but of course, Curtis LeMay, with his cigar, was the center of all the attention.

One night when we were out on one of our many missions we were at Belmar, New Jersey, and some of the gang were kidding me at dinner about my "peanut whistle" out here in Traverse City. Charlie Singer jumped in and said, "Listen, you guys, get off Les's back. He is a manager of a radio station and a principle owner of a radio station, and he hires guys like you. You may come from some of the biggest stations in America, but this guy owns one. So get your facts straight."

The guys kept right on razzing, with the razzing increasing as they had a few more drinks. One of them said, "If you own a radio station, why can't we hear it? It must be only a peanut whistle." Well, by this time it was after midnight. Just for kicks I went to a telephone and I called the people on duty at the station back home in Traverse City. We had a little studio at the transmitter where we could originate transmission and didn't have to go down to the downtown studio. I told them to go on the air with that station to let these boys out here know, by God, that WTCM was for real.

Well, believe it or not, they convinced the boys playing at the Park Place, Joe Dolan's band that night, to come out and broadcast a special tribute at 1:30 in the morning—played a tribute to the boys in the service and dedicated part of it to me there at Belmar, New Jersey. Now this is a long way away, and I don't believe it could happen again in a thousand years, but that station came in there for us at Belmar, New Jersey, as if it was a high-powered local station. I couldn't believe it. From that time on nobody kidded me about the little "peanut whistle" up there in the northwoods.

All this time my devoted wife Anne and young son were living in Philadelphia with Anne's family. It was a relief to know they were comfortable among loved ones.

A very interesting thing happened while I was in Washington, and it might have been a prophetic thing, I don't know. I was given a top-secret job of delivering some military documents. I had an escort with me, a major, and I was put in a seat in a parlor car in a train a half-hour before the train left and told not to leave that seat. But I did not stay; I wandered out onto the station platform and saw a body being wheeled out to be put on the train. I talked to the station master there, whom I knew to be a counterintelligence agent. "What's the idea of the body?" I asked.

He said, "It missed the previous train and we have to stop at West Philadelphia just for an instant to drop the body off." The train that I was on didn't normally stop at West Philadelphia. Well, knowing that it was going to stop there, and knowing that I would be going through there at 5:30 and didn't have to deliver these papers until the next morning, when I could catch another train, I figured I had the evening in Philadelphia, even though I was not supposed to leave that seat on the train.

So I called Bill Kiker, who was at a military base right outside of Philly. I said, "Can you get off? I'd love to see you." He said he thought he could. I told him this train was going to come in, and I'd be in the baggage car and step off when the train stopped. Sure enough, the train stopped at the 30th Street Station. They opened the door, put out the body, and left immediately, leaving me standing on the platform, and there was Bill coming towards me. He had his car and we left the station, and before more than a very few minutes we heard fire engines screaming.

It just so happens that the 30th Street Station is in West Philadelphia, and the Fire Department never has crossed that river except in case of a real catastrophe. If engines were going from there, we knew something terrible had happened. We saw emergency vehicles, ambulances—Bill and I had been chasing emergency vehicles all our lives to see what newsworthy thing might be happening at the other end, and we did so now.

Believe it or not, they were all going to Frankford Junction, and when we got there, too, there was the train that I had been on only a few moments before scattered all over the railroad tracks. Every single person that was in the car that I was in was dead. The major was chewed up like mincemeat. The car broke an axle, jumped the track, and hit a big signal tower, and that tower cut that car open like a watermelon, from one end to the other and halfway through the next car.

There were 108 people killed in that accident in West Philadelphia, and it was one of the worst railway accidents ever in the United States. They announced on the 6:00 news that this accident had taken place in Philadelphia. General George Gordon Meade III, grandson of the George Meade who was the Northern Civil War general, had been one of the people to put me on that train, and he immediately called my in-laws in Philadelphia to tell them that I had been on that train and that someone should go check on the accident. Charlie Singer, also calling at the same time and finding that the number was busy, called Bill Kiker's and told them to go.

So, walking down the railroad tracks in the midst of that unbelievable carnage, I met my father-in-law and Freddy Zierle, my good friend and fellow founder of the station; there I was alive in the midst of all that mess. All around us they were using torches to free the people, taking screaming people out of the wreckage and removing bodies, one of whom surely would have been me. That corpse and the 30th Street Station saved my life, for whatever the future would be.

The experience of working in electronic research during the war, the publications made available to us all, the contacts I met and became conversant with—all of these things broadened my knowledge of electronics to an extent I had never dreamed of. It was a rich and rewarding experience. During the war, as you can see, I did a great deal of travelling. Getting a place to live was a problem, and I rented a room in the Cairo Hotel, which at that time was the tallest building in Washington, D.C. Today it is an old hotel in an old neighborhood, but then it was a pretty nice place, and it wasn't easy to get a room. I had a lawyer friend who owned an interest in that hotel, and he called the manager to get me a space. The manager teamed me up with another guy in a sharing situation, with two beds in the room.

That roomate was Captain Bill Hart, who was a pilot who worked for Pan American Airways. He was a pioneering pilot who had opened up the airways for Pan Am in the Pacific during the late Thirties. An odd thing—after that first night when we shared that room and told each other a little bit about ourselves, we never saw each other during the entire course of the war, even though we shared the same room. I was never there when he was; he was never there when I was. We could see that each other's belongings had been moved about, we could tell that the other guy had been there, but we were seldom in Washington at all, let alone at the same time. We needed to keep that room, though, so we would always have a place to stay.

I left Washington before the end of the war, in 1944, and I felt I had gained so much from my experience. I wish everyone who came home from the war could have felt as if they gained as much from it as I did; it certainly was one of the real learning experiences in my lifetime and may be equal to a Ph.D. in electronics.

CHAPTER FIVE

NORTHWESTERN MICHIGAN COLLEGE

When I came back from the war, I found the station prospering. The predictions I had made for growth in the early days had come true; immediately after the war, came Cadillac, then Alpena, then Gaylord. I had said it would take about ten years to build five stations, and when we dedicated the Gaylord station, Fred Zierle reminded me, "Les, you shouldn't feel so great—you're a month late from what you said we would do back in 1939." So it goes. But I hadn't planned a war in between.

In the town itself, there was a kind of restless spirit about. The cherry industry was looking promising, but it was still a local and state industry. There was a small but active group of business and professional people who wanted to see Traverse City grow; building could commence; industry could happen. How could I and the station take an active role in the growth that was sure to come? I had come back eager to play a part, and I knew the potential of radio to influence change and growth. Seeing the town again re-inspired me. All the things

I had learned in the Army, all the people I had come to know, had given me confidence that radio, and I through it, could play a leadership role in helping the town grow.

I began daily editorials on subjects the town was interested in (or I thought they needed) right after the war, and I continued them into the late 1970's. I believe I editorialized more than any other broadcaster in the country, and I can hope, and certainly do believe, that some good things for the town did come out of it. The power for good in radio and the media in general is tremendous, and I believe in it as firmly now as I did then. Media in any given town should be used to help that town achieve its fullest potential; and that is how I intended to use it as I came back from the war.

Before I left Washington, I was sitting around a table with a bunch of those Ph.D.'s, Dr. Everett and the others, and they were all talking about what they would do after the war was over. I said I had a special idea. One of the things that worried me about Traverse City was that the young people had to leave town to get a higher education or a job. Very few of them stayed around, and one of the most precious commodities a town has is its young people. One of the things Traverse City could do was to have a college, so they would stay right there and put their efforts back into the town. Maybe I could do something to get a college started.

Immediately these college professors had jumped on me. It couldn't be done in that way, they said; founding a college was a lot different from founding a radio station. There is a library, there is certification, there are professors to pay—it is very hard, if not impossible. But I wasn't daunted. The more I looked at the town and envisioned it as the center of a gigantic wheel stretching over five counties, the more I saw a good, thriving college as the hub of that wheel.

So when I returned and got active again in the Chamber of Commerce, the college was on my mind. But I found there was a much more immediate concern for the town, and until it was taken care of, the college couldn't be begun, even as an idea.

It was obvious that something was going to have to be done about Munson, our community hospital. It really had become completely inadequate, by almost everybody's standards. Munson, at that time, was a ward of the State Hospital, training nurses for the hospital. At that time there were seven or eight doctors in Traverse City, most of them surgeons, and they practiced at that hospital, with its one operating room and its small, old-fashioned building with very limited bed space. M.J. MacIntosh, the Oldsmobile dealer and a powerful person at the Traverse City State Bank, was working with a group of doctors to try to get a better facility built as soon as possible. Their goal was $75,000 to build a ward on this hospital to provide extra beds.

In travelling around I had found out what regional hospitals should be, and it seemed to me that that was what we should be talking about—a medical center. I knew several people active with Mayo Clinic in Minnesota, and they said our hospital was totally inadequate, and what we needed here was something completely different. So I met with a committee over at the Park Place, the committee to raise the $75,000. They were negative about the prospects of raising that kind of money in little Traverse City. I wondered how I should start and said, "About this sum of $75,000—I think it's all wrong."

Heads seemed to nod in the group—they all thought it was much too much.

"What I mean is $75,000 is not nearly enough," I continued. "We should raise a half a million and build a real, regional hospital—a medical center with advanced medical treatment equipment." The group was astonished.

The medical practitioners in the area were not behind it, because, I suppose, they could see specialists coming in and taking away their practice. But one man was for it. Frank Power, a fine human being and an outstanding surgeon, backed the project almost as soon as he heard about it. "Let's get going, keep going," was his encouraging advice. Soon we enlisted the aid of Dr. Ed Sladek, the head of the Michigan Medical Society, a Traverse City man.

After many meetings they decided to ask the Kellogg Foundation for help, and that foundation sent up a consultant at their expense to talk about the facility and make a recommendation as to what was needed. They took a survey and determined that it would take three quarters of a million to build the very minimum facility that Traverse City was going to need. Boy, you should have seen that committee. If they couldn't raise $75,000, how could they raise $750,000? But they did get with it, and it was determined to build a good facility. Bob Murchie, Willis Heidbreder, and M.J. MacIntosh, along with Alonzo Wilson of the Traverse City Bank were the real giants of what was to be the Munson Medical Center building effort. (Later Chuck Moorman and Julius "Jake" Beers of that bank continued that support of city projects.)

They hired an architect, developed plans, and decided to raise $600,000. They came to me, then, and asked if I would help in raising the money. It was a knock-em-down-drag-em-out fight to raise the money to build this center. I think I would have dropped out of the fight if it hadn't been for Frank Power; he kept encouraging me to stay in, saying, "You are thinking right. The other facilities are completely inadequate."

The hospital program was started and we raised $600,000, all right. But that wasn't enough, and we had to go back and raise another $200,000, making it a total of $800,000 that was raised. It was a great privilege to have helped organization-wise, through the station, in that drive. One of the most gratifying things was that after the doctors were throughly convinced that the Medical Center concept was correct, they gave fantastically. They really did a great job.

Still, you can see the problem of trying to talk about a college in the midst of all of this. Nobody would have given a plug nickel for a college when we were fighting to bring a decent hospital to the area.

Still, the college inched along, as I was named to head a committee of the Chamber of Commerce (at my suggestion) to investigate plans for a community college in Traverse. I was eager to do something about observations I had been making since I had returned from Washington. First, I had surveyed the territory to see if a college was feasible. I saw that there was nothing north of Mt. Pleasant—where the then Central Michigan College was existing with a rather limited program. I visited lots of colleges as I travelled to extend and supervise the station, and outside of the Upper Peninsula, which was far from us, a huge area seemed in need of a college. Since I had gotten so much from vocational education, I tended in that direction.

As I investigated with the Chamber of Commerce Committee, I found that other people in Traverse had been interested in the intriguing idea of a college here for many years. After World War I, the state legislature had voted to establish a normal school here, but they had not provided funds. In 1940 the Chamber of Commerce had set up a Junior College Committee, including Lars Hochstad, Ben L. Taylor, and Superintendent of Schools, Glenn Loomis. In 1946 Ned Kehoe was in charge of the committee, which included Glenn Loomis, Mrs. Harold Johnson, James T. Milliken; Arnell Engstrom, our state representative; and many others. So there was a good deal of sincere interest.

Meanwhile, our forward-thinking Traverse City public schools had set up an adult education program which had grown in size to 1,500 people in seventy-two classes by 1951. People did want to go on with their education; all they needed was a place. A college for Traverse City became the primary interest of my life. The college, I thought, would become the focal point for growth and education in all northwest Michigan, a suitable companion to the newly constructed Munson Medical Center.

I began to talk to Arnell Engstrom and others about seriously establishing the college. The first hurdle was to get the Michigan Legislature to change the law to permit communities of under 25,000 people to finance and operate a college. Bill Number 380 took care of that, and I really must say that Arnell Engstrom showed his strength here, as he worked to get this through the legislature. It became a cause with me at that level too; it seemed to me that the legislature and everybody, for that matter, short-changed northwestern Michigan. North of Town Line Sixteen, an area of 350,000, very little seemed done for the people. In the U.P., an area in total of 250,000, there were already colleges flourishing. Our time had come.

It seemed to me and the others I was talking to that it would take $250,000 to get this college off the ground. It was unthinkable to me that we should use local tax dollars to begin this school; we would have to nickel-and-dime it. The kickoff meeting was held January 24, 1951, at the Chamber of Commerce. I had asked all of the life insurance agents in Traverse City to come, and I think all of them did. H. Neal Jones was president of the Northern Michigan Association of Life Underwriters, and I said to him and the others, "You guys are the best people for selling something that I know of, and I want to convince you that you should sell this college idea to the public here in the city. Let's get started with a Founders' Club. If you can get 400 people to put $100 on the line, we will have a starting sum to jump off with. $40,000 will see us a long way on the road to this college."

Lo and behold, they did this—they got 400 people to put down $100, and the Founders' Club was born. We gave each of these people or businesses a plaque, and if you visit these businesses today, you will see Founders' Plaques for Northwestern Michigan College on the wall.

That was some drive; I will never forget it; and it was made more interesting and significant by the fact that not all the contributions, by any means, were $100—some were more, some less. Everybody started getting on the bandwagon, with the station back of it, naturally, and I wore a sign around that said, "Pin a buck on me for NMC." (That was what it was going to be called, although I had originally favored Traverse City College or something like that for the name.)

The Independent Grocer's Alliance gave a penny for each loaf of bread housewives bought, keeping cannisters by their checkout counters. Child Study Club Six donated the proceeds of a dance they held at the Park Place. The group from the Little Theater made $380 on a performance of *Peter Pan*, and a little girl came to make the presentation. One of the most important efforts came from a man who was to become one of the solidest and best supporters of NMC—Gerald Oleson. He sponsored a "Fisharee" at his trout pond; people in the town could fish for trout and donate ten cents an inch to the new college. Some of the fishermen got together and planned a dinner at Pete Baksakis's new Inn for the benefit of the college; they fished and the public came to eat. Over $1,600 was raised at that trout supper for the college in September.

Meanwhile, we were moving forward rapidly with plans to really open. In June, when we knew we had $30,000 and that the bill had passed the Michigan legislature (30-1 in the Senate, on May 16), we began asking for students and began hiring teachers.

That bill was a landmark, and it set the stage for later legislation (which I also worked hard on) which would set up Michigan's community college system. The 1951 bill allowed cities of our size to set up colleges under the supervision of the local superintendents of schools. Local units of government could give financial support to these colleges, and they would be recognized for official state aid.

I was on the school board of the city of Traverse City—and the school board, according to that legislation, took over the management of the college that would be underway shortly. I didn't really approve of that, but there it was. I thought it should be completely independent with its own board. Later, we amended the act and made it possible for the school to be administered by a separate board, and the Board of Trustees of Northwestern Michigan College was born, in 1955. I was elected chairman, a post I held for twenty-two years.

Financially, the school was now being funded by Educational Fund, Incorporated, a source outside of the public money, which had done the original fund-raising for the Founders' Club and was continuing to make plans for buildings and also to raise more money to insure the college's first year and its

The author

The Biederman family after World War II: (left to right) Ross, Paul, Anne, and Les.

Virginia Halsal became the World War II pinup sweetheart of soldiers from Traverse City in a WTCM newsletter promotion effort.

Les Biederman with David Sarnoff, president of RCA.

A 1951 fund-raising effort for the new college was a fisharee. Shown here are Arnell Engstrom and Peter Baksakis.

Following the fisharee, Traverse City people ate fish in another fund-raiser at Pete Baksakis's restaurant.

D. B. Steinman, the designer of the Mackinac Bridge, received a Wolverine Frontiersman Award from Michigan's Governor G. Mennen Williams on the same day the author received his award.

Volunteers helped ready the airport buildings in Traverse City for Northwestern Michigan College, when it opened in 1951.

Buildings at the airport were the college's first home.

Ground breaking for the first permanent buildings at the college with Harlan Hatcher, president of the University of Michigan, and the author.

Dismantled Coast Guard buildings became college buildings in 1955 after the move to the campus.

The first of many very successful college barbeques, May 27, 1956.

Commencement, 1955, with Les Biederman, chairman of the Board of Trustees of Northwestern Michigan College, at the podium.

The Board of Trustees of Northwestern Michigan College in the 1960's.

American Cable Network.

Traverse City Cherry Queen Julie Ann Hamilton brought a ton of fudge to the Philadelphia Naval Hospital in 1969 as a part of the Allegheny adventure.

Breaking ground for the Mark Osterlin Library. Les Biederman manning a huge excavator.

The Allegheny.

The Happy Days.

future. There were teachers to be hired, students to be enrolled and—where in the world were we going to put them? We had about three months to figure all these "details" out.

Just about every day I was editoralizing on the station, and the money was continuing to come in. There was a woman named Mrs. Brown who made an apron with a patch on it. She put a dollar in the patch and passed it from house to house around Torch Lake, asking the grandmothers there to put a penny on the apron for every year they had been on the earth. She raised hundreds of dollars for the college that way. It wasn't just the money, of course, as they say, but the idea that scores of people like her were thinking of this as their college and realizing what the institution would do for the whole area, and then doing their part. It made quite a difference. It has been said that Northwestern Michigan College was a college "of the people, by the people, for the people;" and this is right. I'm not sure everyone knows it was the first community college in Michigan, and it truly came out of community effort.

Jerry Oleson didn't just stop at his trout pond idea. He had a sandwich luncheon at his Garfield store and raised another $1,200. That was another shot in the arm. We also had a bake sale. Everybody thought it was a joke—us having a bake sale for the college like a bunch of kids. But we convinced a manufacturer of box cakes to give the mix to a lot of people; and they made up the cakes and took them to a place of exchange and we sold the cakes for $1.00. That raised $1,400.

But selling cakes didn't provide a temporary home for the college, and time was running out. The committee said Oak Park School was vacant and thought it would be adequate. It was a very old school, and some of the rooms were in the basement. I didn't think that would work very well. On one of the trips I made, though, I saw the airport building on Airport Road. The City Commission had control of that building, with Capital Airlines using part of the space. So the Board of Education leased it to the Educational Fund without charge, and the city, to show their backing, provided heat and electricity. We had a building.

Actually, plans for a permanent building had begun much earlier, when we first got serious about the idea of a college. I looked around and saw that there was a big, beautiful piece of property for sale across from the fairgrounds. I bargained and bargained, really, as a private person who hoped it could become official; and I eventually put my own money on the line for an option. We bought the original property for $40,000 and bought some additional land for $7,500 adjacent to it. That later piece was a swamp, which doesn't exist now. As plans for buying that property were underway, a group of architects from Traverse pooled their resources and went to work for us. Hartford Field was the chairman, and Gordon Cornwell, Orus Eash and Ralph Bauer Associates worked with him. They planned a building in the neighborhood of $350,000, but of course we couldn't hope for something like that for a while. Meanwhile, we had the old administration building at the airport to get ready; the forty or so students who signed up by August, would be coming, the deadline fast drawing near.

We called for a crew of volunteers to get this ramshackle old building ready for students in a very short time. Plumbers, volunteer carpenters, painters—it seemed like most of Traverse City was working on the building at one time or another. A local hardware dealer sanded and refinished the floors. All in all, 218 volunteers worked four days and it cost us—would you believe it, $34. Most everything was donated.

September 17, 1951, Preston Tanis, the newly hired director, opened the college to the sixty-five students we now had. On the first faculty were Marcus Sheffer, psychology; Walt Beardsley, history and economics; Ellis Wunsch, English and humanities; Pauline Bauer, business ed.; Velma Brand, Spanish and biology; and Harry Strauss, librarian. I was convinced they were as good a faculty as that of any other little college in the state.

By January the college had expanded the very basic first curriculum to include world civilization, sociology, shorthand, typing, college bookkeeping, and machine shop (I was glad about that). We got a snack bar going, so the kids could eat right there "on campus." I was really pushing for more vocational offerings, because I thought this was mostly where the future of the college lay. The Kellogg Foundation had sent a bunch of us out West to see community colleges, and we had been impressed. Some of the most successful had what they called an "upside down" philosophy—they put vocational training first.

Soon some surplus buildings came our way, and it was a stroke of good fortune that they did. Four Coast Guard buildings still stood after World War II, and we purchased them from the Federal Security Agency through the services of Representative Ruth Thompson. They cost $6,000, but we got them for $300. This was a ninety-nine percent discount. We sat down with John Norton, who was an engineer and architect, and Bill Comstock, who was a contractor; and found a way to take those buildings apart and build a temporary college facility on our new site across from the fairgrounds. Lo and behold, we built an eight-room college out of those buildings on what is now the campus.

The earth-turning ceremony was June 3, 1952, and I was supposed to get somebody to turn the ceremonial shovelful. I thought about it at home the night before, and I called Harlan Hatcher, president of the University of Michigan, at his home in Ann Arbor. I wasn't sure if he would honor us; his wife had thought he would come. I ran out and bought a shiny shovel for him to use, and sure enough, the next day he came not only to turn the shovelful but also to make a speech.

A new campaign had to be launched, of course, to raise money for erecting the new facility. The second year at the college we had 134 students from Cheboygan, Petoskey, Grayling and other "far-flung" spots; and we now had 2,150 adults taking extension courses that we had developed with larger schools in the state. We were going to need good, well-utilized space.

Paul Gustafson chaired a campaign to raise $150,000, and I hoped it would go as well as it needed to. Again, my faith in the community was rewarded: by January 12, we had $53,000; by January 30, $104,372 was in hand. We began work in earnest to transform those old Coast Guard buildings into a full-fledged college.

Arms and Cole was one of the standouts I recall in the work on this building. They put the heating plant in; we bought the material. We had all the radiators and piping from the old buildings as we tore them down, but it wasn't much material. We got a used boiler from the Hillsdale Hospital, and we sent a cherry truck to load it on down there and bring it up. Then a group of rural masons came from Alden and Rapid City to build the building for the heating plant, so the college could be in business. We weren't connected with the city sewers, so we had to build a septic tank. As luck would have it, a truck ran over the septic tank and crushed in the top of it; we had a terrible mess on our hands.

Yes, it was a tremendous lot of work and trouble, but wasn't it worth doing? Here we have a college with 3,500 daytime students in 1982, and 4,500 students at night, thousands and thousands of graduates, some with Ph.D's, and some now teaching at the college; it was worth all the trouble, yes, all.

We had these two buildings, each with four classrooms in them with a corridor connecting them that was 300 feet long. We had a little dinette alongside of it; we conned the company that manufacturers National Cash Registers into giving us a cash register for the thing. Milliken's Department Store laid the linoleum in that mini-cafeteria. Purvis Brothers got their men to volunteer the big smokestack; we really had more wheeling and dealing and fixing up than you can possibly imagine to get that place open, but we did get it built.

When the college moved, March 3, 1955, to the present campus, the students moved everything. We had some volunteers with trucks, and on a Saturday the whole college, including faculty, students, and some people from the town—everybody—moved desks, 4,000 books, and all, to the new 140-acre campus. It took twelve of those trucks.

Then we had the problem of designing and building the first permanent building, which we are still using today, the administration building. John Norton designed it, and my friend Bob Matthews who owned a company which made pre-cast concrete joists, worked with us and soon the building was up too, costing less than $100,000. Before that building went up, Reed Chapin, who was then the treasurer of the college and a member of the Board of Trustees, said, "You know how much it cost to build this college?" and he answered that we had $37,500 invested, at that time, for a college of 300. So many people donated so much to create and establish this college. I recall that we needed structural steel to build this first facility, and we couldn't afford it. Word got to the company that was furnishing the structural steel that we were having trouble raising money, and Betty Jervis, the president of that company, presented us with a check to pay for the steel we bought from her company. We bought the steel; they presented us with a check to pay for it.

Sometime during this period the Student Council wanted to raise some money for their operations, and Jimmy DeLappis, a student from Baltimore, who was involved with the Student Council, planned a spaghetti supper. He made spaghetti by the ton, and it was served on classroom tables in the corridor, 300 feet long twelve feet wide. Dinner in a hall; we really packed them in. Jim DeLappis is one of our favorite college alums; he is very successful today.

We have had some real giants in community leadership on the board of the college, and I certainly am glad we didn't settle for letting the school board run the college. People like Arnell Engstrom, Andy Olson, Dr. Weitz; George Altonburg, who taught at Highland Park Community College; but of all the people who have supported the college from Day One, Jerry and Frances Oleson stand out as the finest. Each year they sponsor the college barbcquc, which has raised in excess of half a million dollars for the college. We have fed as many as 14,000 people in one day at that popular event. I still have a whistle presented to us by Consulting Engineer Stewart Long, which I blow for each 1,000 people served; and I have had to blow it often in recent years. Jerry Oleson and his wife Frances donate all the food to this tremendous event, and all the proceeds go to the college. I don't believe that college would be there and be as successful as it is, if it hadn't been for the financial and moral support these people have given. Without them and the hundreds of others who have made so many fine and varied contributions through the years in differing ways, we would not have been able to have this college "of the people, by the people, for the people."

Although we had done pretty well with our first little library, it was my big dream to have a fine library for the college. We had a campaign and raised a couple of hundred thousand dollars, and as a result the Mark Osterlin Library stands at the college. Now it, too, is too small, and we need other facilities to go with the library, so the college is going to be getting busy and building a bigger library in the future.

When we said we were going to establish a college, Grand Traverse County had given us $30,000. Leelanau County gave us $9,000. When the time came for the library, I went around to all the townships in the five-county area, and all the townships except for two made a contribution for that library from their township funds. If you check the rosters of the college, you will see students come from all of those townships; so we hope they have gotten their money's worth.

* * * *

The college wasn't the only thing that happened in the Fifties to me and the town. In the early 1950's the Parsons Company occupied a site at the foot of Division Street, where it meets the Bay. On this site had originally been the Johnson-Randall Furniture Factory. Now the state was going to build a boulevard there, so a problem arose: where do we get a new plant for Parsons? John Parsons met with the Chamber of Commerce and told them what he needed, so we decided to create an industrial fund to not only help this plant but stimulate industry in the region.

I knew that Altoona, Pennsylvania had a going industrial fund, so to Altoona I went, and I learned about raising money and so forth. I came back and called a meeting at the Park Place. The Parsons Company represented about 300 jobs, making helicopter rotor blades, and they did not have the backing alone to build a new plant. An industrial fund could build a plant for such a company as Parsons and then rent it to stimulate jobs and industry in the community; and it was this format that was adopted, patterned after the Altoona enterprise.

First the committee sent me to Philadelphia to visit with Frank Piasakie, the helicopter designer, to see if this was a legitimate venture for coming years; Frank knew John Parsons and assured me it was a good risk. John Parsons acquired some real estate at Three Mile Road, and we officially created the Traverse City Industrial Fund. Bob Murchie drew up the papers, and I was elected president, a position I occupied for eleven years.

We built that Parsons Plant, and they paid the industrial fund a lot of money in rent for the use of that building; a large fund was built up, and it has been used to operate the industrial fund to this day. While we were in the midst of the Parsons project, Tim O'Connor came to us. He had a little machine shop, and he needed $9,000 to acquire a machine shop and get his business booming. He got it. Then there were two Greek boys who came down from Elk Rapids. They were using a couple of private garages to bake pies from recipes their dad had created when he had sold baked goods. They wanted to build a plant to bake their apple and pumpkin delicacies; they needed so much money, they said. There was some federal funding available, but they wanted to apply to the industrial fund for help. There was a lot of argument back and forth; not everybody wanted to back these two boys. But we did, and today Chef Pierre ships those pies all over the world; Pete Dendrinos and Mike Denos have built a company that employs 900 people in Traverse City and had, recently, a hundred million dollar year of business sales.

The Traverse City Industrial Fund has built dozens of buildings and established many businesses in Traverse City; there are thousands of people employed in these businesses now. I never will forget those years when we seemed always to be raising money. Everybody had his money involved. I remember Jerry Oleson saying he would go out and raise $15,000, or something of the sort, and two days later he walked in and laid the money on the table. Jerry Oleson is an exceptional guy in so many ways.

And, of course, there were some interesting personal stories from the time of the Fifties. One of them concerns a sturgeon, and I still chuckle about it when I think of it.

In the area of Cheboygan there is a wintertime fishing sport known as spearing for sturgeon. Now a sturgeon is a great fish anywhere from four to seven feet long and weighing anywhere from sixty to 150 pounds. The fishermen cut a hole in the ice and spear the fish through this opening. There aren't too many of the fish, but there are enough to make it a fascinating challenge, a great sport.

Many of the people in the Petoskey, Harbor Springs, and Cheboygan areas go sturgeon-spearing, and one of my acquaintances got fascinated by the whole idea. Herman Kays of Petoskey, who owned a finance company and made small loans, was in Cheboygan and saw a man who had caught a sturgeon that weighed 105 pounds and was six foot five in length. He bought it from the man, paying $100. He took this fish down to Petoskey and started bragging the way he sometimes did about the fish that *he* had speared. Unbeknownst to Herman, the man who had caught the fish had kept a small "V" of the tail when he had sold the fish, clipping it off with a little pair of scissors and keeping it as a memento of his big catch.

Now there had been a feud going on in Petoskey for years between the editor of the newspaper there, Dick Allgire, and Herman Kays. Dick would frequently make statements about Herman Kays in the *News Review* there, say things that were not always a credit to Herman. When Herman began noising it around that he had caught this marvelous fish, Dick Allgire decided to do a little bit of investigating and he went up to Cheboygan and found the man who had sold the fish to Herman. He bought the little piece of the fish's tail from the man and he returned to Petoskey, sure that he had caught Herman, whom he disliked intensely, in a colossal lie that would discredit him forever. He demanded that Herman produce the fish.

All of this had happened, and I did not know about it; but on a Saturday who should come into my office but Herman. He sat there and said he had to commit suicide. He had been challenged to produce this fish. Although he didn't know that this man did have a piece of the fish's tail, he believed he could be proved to be a liar, and he would be in disgrace. He whipped a pistol out of his pocket and was about to blow his brains out. I dove across the desk, wrestled with him for the pistol; the pistol went off and sent a bullet into the door frame, but I finally did get the pistol away from Herman. It took me about a half hour or so to get him cooled off, and we talked about what could be done.

Some way what we needed to do was to get another fish so that the story couldn't be traced back. He said there was no possible way to get another sturgeon like that. So I got on the phone and called friends of mine up in the lakes of Minnesota; and we couldn't get a sturgeon like that, sure enough. Four feet, five feet, but not six feet long. Somebody told me that they were catching Atlantic sturgeon off the East Coast; they were supposed to be like the Great Lakes version. So I called one of my cousins back at good old Cape May and he said, "Yes, it was true, the Atlantic sturgeon is very large, but they were not running off Cape May but instead off Cape Hatteras. So I contacted Johnny Elmer at WCBM in Baltimore, and he put me in touch with some people down in that area. They said there would be a possibility of getting one of these fish.

So Herman and I got into his car and we drove down to Belhaven, North Carolina, where a lot of fishing boats put in. We got in touch with a man by the name of Anson Smith, who owns a fishing fleet. Anson got on the radio and said there was a $500 bonus for anybody who would bring in a sturgeon weighing 105 pounds and six feet five long. We had a lot of radio traffic, one guy calling saying, "I've got one so big," another, "I have one twelve foot long. How much do I get for that?"

After several days of this, a guy called in on the radio saying, "I've got your fish." Herman was in ecstasy; now he would have a fish that would be his own. There was a problem; the Atlantic sturgeon, it turns out, is red. Not only that, but the Atlantic sturgeon has three feelers off its chin; the Great Lakes one had four. So it seemed it wouldn't work.

Well, I got the old gray matter working, and I remembered the curator of the commercial museum in Philadelphia was an old neighbor of mine—I didn't even remember his name. I called the commercial museum and I located the man. He said, "Bring the fish up and I'll fix it." So we loaded the fish in the car and headed with it to Philadelphia.

When we got there, my friend was ready for us. He had a cow trough (like what cows drink out of) filled with dye, and he dyed the fish black. It turned out beautifully. Then he cut off the three feelers and inserted four plastic feelers. Now we had a fish that looked exactly right.

But now we also had the problem of getting that fish home. I thought a bit and contacted an undertaker friend of mine who gave us a rough box, a shipping box for coffins. We lined the box with oilcloth, filled it with ice, put the fish in, put the lid on, and shipped it to Traverse City.

When that fish arrived in Traverse on the express truck, Herman and I were there. We got the fish out of the box and because there was still ice in it, it was in good shape. It was, however, as stiff as a piece of wood. We put it in his car with the tail sticking out and Herman headed for Petoskey at 3:00 in the morning. As luck would have it, when he reached Atwood, he got stopped by a policeman for speeding. He talked his way out of the ticket, but the policeman asked about the fish. Herman said he was on his way home from the Sportsman's Show in Chicago, and now he was going home with it.

When he got back home, he told everybody he was ready to show the fish. It was put out on the table at the Elks Club, and almost everyone in Petoskey came to see that fish. Old Dick Allgire arrived ready for the kill, with the piece of the tail ready to match it with Herman's fish, but he couldn't find the place it was cut out. In the meantime, Herman had buried the original fish in his garage. I had helped him.

Well, everybody was happy. Glad to see the fish, they congratulated Herman. The next day Dick Allgire apologized in the paper, saying he had been given bad information. I wasn't happy though; when they had shown the fish at the Elks Club that afternoon they had decided to cook the fish and have a dinner at the Elks Club Thursday night. I was scared to death that people would kick the bucket as a result of the dye, but it all went well, and that was the end of the episode—for then.

Some ten or so years later I was in Clare, Michigan at the Dougherty Hotel. Ken Thompson and I were on a business trip, and a terrible storm was brewing; we thought if we stopped for dinner, maybe the storm would ease up a little. Ken asked me to tell him the sturgeon story, and so I did, in all its lurid details. When I had finished, a guy from the booth in back of us jumped up and yelled, "Why you dirty so-and-so, so that's how you did it. I thought you had something to do with that. So that's how I was conned!" Who was it? Why it was Dick Allgire, the editor of the Petoskey newspaper, who now works for United States Steel.

Another story I should put in here is the story of how the church at Alba burned. Here is how it goes. For a number of years, I have been a member of the board of the Scenic Trails Council of the Boys Scouts of America. One time there were some problems over in Alpena, and the Boy Scout executive

Pop Warner asked several of us on the board to go with him to clear them up. I don't recall exactly who was in that car—I think the Traverse City optometrist Ken Tinker was there, I know Pop was there. I think there were five of us. We had gone over for a Saturday dinner meeting, stayed the night, and were coming back. We came to the little town of Alba, and was it ever cold! Thirty below zero, they were announcing, and the old smoke was going straight up from the chimneys the way it does when it is awfully cold.

We got to Alba and I said, "Wait a minute, there's something wrong over there. There's some smoke or fog coming out from under the eaves." As soon as we got close to the church, we could smell it. That church was on fire, with the congregation inside singing away on hymns. I walked right in the church and went up to the front and said to the minister, "Get these people out of here, this church is on fire!" He said, "No," but he did it anyway.

So everybody went out, and we started carrying out the pews and then the song books and the Bibles and everything that was in there, and it was hotter than hell. The fire was in the walls of the church, and it was just ready to break out. When it did, we all had to get out and stay out.

I had a two-way radio in the car, and I called the station at Petoskey and said we needed some volunteer help to fight the fire; they in turn called our Traverse City and Gaylord stations. "Bring water to fight the fire," they said. It was rather amusing and sad, really, to see those trucks come up and start to squirt water. By the time it hit the building in that freezing weather, it was solid ice. The pumps froze up; you never saw such a mess. We just stood there and watched that church burn down. You should have seen the mobs. Everybody had heard the messages on the radio; nobody was there to fight the fire, much, as far as I could see. They were there to see the fire.

Alba, Elmira, Mancelona fire departments were there, but there wasn't anything to be done. I'll never forget that sickening sound when that bell fell out of the belfry and went through to the basement. I was wearing a fur hat on my head, I recall it well. I took that fur hat off my head, and I put a twenty dollar bill in it. I said, "We've all had a lot of excitement; we've seen the church burn, and now let's help these people build a new church." I collected over $1,000 in a few minutes.

I didn't know what to do with the money and didn't know where to find the people to give it to. I did know where the telephone exchange was around there, so I took the money over to it and dumped it on the floor. I said, "Here, tell the people in the church that we want to help them build a new one."

Two years later as I was pinning a badge on a Boy Scout from Scenic Trails Council, I saw he was staring at me. "You're the man. You're the man who raised the money for the Alba Church," he said. It had just so happened that they had insurance money of $7,000 on the church. They also had a $7,000 mortgage on the church, so that when this was paid off, they were wiped out. Being elderly people, mostly, in the church, it seemed for them an impossible job to build a new church; but the fact that some strangers had provided the first gift on that night the church burned down had been such a shot in the arm for them that they got a fund drive going.

The little area rallied. Orville Walker, a farmer in the area, gave them the potatoes off ten acres and other farmers did the same. They got busy and raised about $35,000 and built a new brick church. About a month after I pinned that metal on that boy, I got a telephone call from the preacher, asking me to come to a dinner in that new church. It was quite a thrill to go out there and see that new brick church and think of all the people who had a part, even if they didn't much intend to, in getting it started.

CHAPTER SIX

THE MARITIME ACADEMY AND THE SIXTIES

By 1960 the Paul Bunyan Network was rounded out with the addition of television and, eventually, cable TV. After we had the five radio stations completed, we had looked around to see what we should do next, and it seemed inevitable that we should go in the direction of TV.

We were, by now, affiliated with NBC. We had joined the Mutual Network in 1944, and five years later had gone with the growing NBC system, which was a pioneering giant in TV work. I had had long-standing relationships with various people at RCA before we had gone with the network, as a matter of fact. I had become acquainted with David Sarnoff, who was also a wireless man in the Thirties, when I was frequently at the Camden, New Jersey, operation of RCA. Many research engineers were there, and we all knew each other. In those early days, radio people were all one family. Andrew Ingliss, now the president of RCA Satellite Communications, was also an acquaintance of mine from the early days. He was from Petoskey, Michigan, but I did not know him there. I met him during the war, when he was a consulting engineer for the government and was advising for our work.

At seminars and conventions, where I would keep up with the latest projects and enterprises of Sarnoff and the others at RCA, television advances were often discussed, as this infant industry began to get off the ground. I met Andy Hammerschmidt, an important executive in the development of color TV, and Bob Shelby of RCA, who really developed the present color system we now use in TV.

As we were investigating how we might get into TV, the Spartan Company of Jackson, Michigan, announced that they were going to build a television station in Cadillac. We thought we'd better get on the ball, fast. We filed an application for a TV station; the Jackson outfit was first, and we were second. That was in 1954.

Subsequently there was a question about how you cover additional areas, and we built a complete TV station in Cheboygan. We were really fearful that we couldn't support ourselves in Cheboygan, and, in fact, that did prove to be the case. We lost a lot of money on that venture, and then we made it a satellite, the two stations running the same program at the same time.

Then the Cadillac station was being out-rated, because we had viewers that they couldn't reach; so they built a station in the Upper Peninsula at Gatesville. That's how they got to be Channels Nine and Ten, Cadillac and Gatesville, and we got to be Seven in Traverse City and Channel Four in Cheboygan.

I enjoyed getting around a lot in the broadcasting industry in those days, and my associations with NBC people were very interesting. Morgan Beatty, a distinquished newsman for NBC for many years, was a close friend and associate. Pauline Fredericks, the U.N. correspondent, often briefed me in the newsroom at the U.N. She introduced me to Dag Hammarskjold and Jacob Malik. I was the northern Michigan correspondent for NBC News, and at times sent on-the-spot reports. One, I recall, was from Copemish, where a terrible nine-fatality accident made the weekend news. I broadcast it from my car.

I watched Tom Brokaw come through the ranks and almost hired Tom Pettit, one of the best of NBC's present correspondents, to be the news director at WTCM. I knew David Brinkley also, but the person I knew best of all was Chet Huntley. His wife Tippy was the daughter of a good friend of mine, Art Stringer, also in the broadcasting industry. (I think I may have introduced Chet to Tippy, but I'm not sure.)

By 1965 and 1966 cable TV was getting to be important. We saw some people who were coming up with some real schlock proposals for a three-channel cable television system in Traverse City; and one outfit came up with one for a five-channel system. It just so happened, that as a boy I grew up with Milton Chapp in Philadelphia, and he was a real entrepreneur, and is now in the cable television industry; he developed the equipment and system which was successful. I knew they had a twelve-channel system. I went before the City Commission and applied for a franchise. We had two competitors, one promoting the three-channel system, the other the five-channel system. We proposed a Jerrold twelve-channel setup; they granted us a franchise, and we built the cable television network.

In the Sixties, I was continuing to be involved in Traverse City's growth. Daily the station would take some point of view on some subject, or rather I would. It varied a lot; usually a couple of hundred documents a week would cross my desk in the studio, on every subject from moonshine to moonlandings. There I sat reading as I puffed away on the cigars that seemed to have become my trademark since the Fifties, when I started smoking them; most often I would find something to get excited about editorializing about.

The ski industry was getting going; they needed a boost on the air. Traverse City High School was having projects and needed some positive publicity. The government in Washington, the local boys in Traverse City government, the cherry industry—I saw everybody as fair game, and each day a new opportunity to try to help something fairly positive happen.

Here are a couple of editorials from the Sixties.

May 31, 1967

THE UPPER PENINSULA IS DEVELOPING ALSO

During the past several days, it was the privilege of your editor to pay a visit to the Upper Peninsula. The last time that we visited Iron Mountain was shortly after the Ford woodworking plant had been shut down. The town was really in trouble.

Today, visiting the same city is different. There is lots of activity. The tourist industry has increased, as attested by the number of fine new motels and eating establishments. There is also some additional mining activity. Everyone is bridge-conscious. They resent the high tolls and feel that the state should in some way subsidize the cost of the maintenance and bonds on the bridge. For instance, in discussing this with an industrial representative, he pointed out that his company truck must pay $25 for each way for a total of $50 per round trip.

This company is in the wood products business, treating wooden poles for sale to the utilities for power and telephone lines. With this $50 surcharge on shipping costs, they find it very difficult to compete with the Alabama suppliers, who have a much lower labor cost. The cost of unemployment insurance and workman's compensation in Michigan is much greater than in the South, and as a result the labor cost is about half of the cost in Michigan. In addition, such a plant must shut down for four months in the year due to weather. The southern mills do not have this problem. As a result, the utility companies in Michigan and Wisconsin spend much of their money in the southern states rather than in Michigan.

All in all, however, it was a nice experience to see the fine new homes and other facilities that have been constructed in the past five years. Also, both the State and Federal Government have done a great deal in developing parks and other recreation facilities. The Upper Peninsula is now on its way and has a splendid future.

Thursday, November 2, 1967

WE ARE GETTING MORE HORSES, NOT ONLY IN OUR CARS

It looks as though the horse is upstaging the automobile and boat in the American family recreation scene. While no accurate count is available, the number of pleasure horses from Maine to California has been estimated from five to seven million. There are plenty around Traverse City.

The last U.S. horse census made in 1959 showed nearly three million horses and mules—mostly on farms. The greatest increase today is around the major population centers.

The 4-H Clubs have been one of the most enthusiastic boosters of the pleasure horse. Recent horse shows and fairs have featured 4-H owners and riders who have claimed their share of honors and trophies.

The national 4-H horse program last year headed the list for enrollment increase in thirty-two major 4-H award programs supervised by the Cooperative Extension Service. The horse program gained more than 19,000 new members—bringing the 1966 total to over 165,000.

The young horsemen learn much more than to mount and ride. They learn how to judge horses—to select proper equipment and keep them in good condition. Horse science projects cover anatomy, nutrition, disease, and reproduction. Members are coached in show-ring performance and responsibility for the horses.

The 4-H Horse program is sponsored nationally by Merck & Co., Inc. of Rahway, New Jersey. Last year a Puerto Rican boy received one of the $500 scholarships offered in the program. The five other recipients were from Idaho, Indiana, Iowa, Pennsylvania, and Texas. They were all girls.

Monday, November 6, 1967

PUERTO RICO IS A PART OF THE UNITED STATES

Last week, it was the honor of your editor to attend a meeting of the NBC management on the Island of Puerto Rico. The meeting took place in the Americana Hotel in San Juan. It was quite an experience and our first visit to the Islands of the Caribbean.

In our spare time it would have been possible and perhaps even advisable to lounge around the pool soaking up the sun, or perhaps in the several bars of the hotel, or perhaps in the gambling casino which was in full operation.

However, inasmuch as we were there, we tried to use our free time to learn something of the island and its people. This is a territory of the United States, and one day will no doubt become our 51st State.

The people of this island are every color from blue-black to white. They are all mixed up. They are happy people. At least they appear so. Never did we see so many transistor radios, all playing Mexican music.

Spanish is the language, and it is hard to find people that can understand even a smattering of English. As a result, communication is difficult, particularly in the rural areas.

This island is very mountainous. They have excellent roads down in the flatlands, but when you get on the mountains, it is like the goat trails in the Himalayas. And, all over these mountains, people live. This is a very crowded place.

Without a question the poverty there is about as bad as anywhere, and we are sending billions of dollars there to help improve conditions. We will tell you about some of these activities in later editorials. This week, you will hear much about the little jewel Puerto Rico.

One of the projects of the Sixties involved a sort of eccentric, but fascinating hobby I've had for most of my life—the subject of Pitcairn Island. When I'd been at Cooke Junior High an English teacher of mine, Mr. Glassman, gave me a research project that took me to the Philadelphia Public Library downtown to research a certain subject in the old newspapers file. I was to read a certain clipping and write about it in my own words, which I did.

This particular subject was in a turn-of-the-century paper; and as I read, I found my eyes lit on an article about another subject—Pitcairn Island. The article said that some sailors had been marooned on an island named, I think, Henderson Island, near Pitcairn. The people from Pitcairn had come over to cut wood and found two nearly emaciated men who had been staying alive by eating native vegetation and a few fish.

The Pitcairn men had taken the shipwrecked sailors back to their home isle and probably saved their lives; this was what the article stated.

I began thinking about what it would be to live on an island, and got curious about just where and what Pitcairn Island was. I hit the atlases and found out it was a tiny island two miles long and a mile wide that rises out of the Pacific about 1,000 miles southeast of Tahiti. It is about sixty miles from Henderson Island, and the Pitcairn people had crossed that distance across the open sea. What kind of people would make that sort of trip to cut wood, I wondered.

I got curious as the dickens about Pitcairn Island and found out that it was the spot which became the refuge and final home of the mutineers who had taken over *HMS Bounty* in the late 1700's. Some of the officers and men of the ship had taken the ship from the infamous Captain Bligh after his behavior became so cruel that it was intolerable. Then, after having set Captain Bligh and some of the loyal sailors adrift in an open boat, they had proceeded, under the leadership of officer Fletcher Christian, to seek out a home, and had found Pitcairn Island.

But what had happened after that, I wondered, and sent a letter to the island to find out. I wrote, "Head Man, Pitcairn Island, Pacific Ocean." In the letter I asked whether any of the descendents of the *Bounty* crew were still there, and if so, what they were doing. I thought I might never get an answer back, but lo and behold, who should write back but Andrew Young, who said he was the chief of the island's nine-man council. He told me that Fletcher Christian and all the men on the *Bounty* who had settled on Pitcairn Island had married native girls in Tahiti, and all of the present 110 inhabitants were direct descendents of these *Bounty* crewmen and their native wives.

This began a fifty-five year correspondence between me and the people on that island. I found out they farmed small plots, and depended a good deal on wild goats and pigs, that were descendents of *Bounty* stock. They also sold postage stamps from their faraway island, as well as baskets and fruit which they brought out to the occasional boats which stopped at the island. In this way, they made a simple living.

I became involved in getting ham radio to Pitcairn, so that ham operators all over the world could talk to that romantic spot. Don Wallace (call letters W-6 AM), who lived in California, sponsored a campaign through the American Relay League and *QST* magazine to acquire equipment to get a rig going. Wally Watt, who became executive vice-president of RCA, and I were also involved, although I did not actually go to the island when it was time to get the equipment going.

I kept in contact through ham radio, and in the Sixties I was writing to Parkin Christian, a direct descendent of Fletcher, and Andrew Young, now an old man. I always asked the islanders if there was anything I or the town where I lived could do for them—anything they couldn't get there. Andrew Young wrote me that they needed work pants, shirts, and cloth. I wrote saying we would help. Over the radio we made an appeal for shoes, clothing, cloth, needles—everything the islanders said they were in need of.

The thing took off. J.C. Penney gave us twenty pairs of shears and other companies gave nails, hinges, tools, and other items. Some people wanted to contribute money, and we got the word around a bit. David Sarnoff put his name on the contributors' list along with movie stars Robert Taylor, Chuck Connors, and Marjorie Lord. Most of the donors, though, were Traverse City folks. Now the question was, how do we get all this stuff to Pitcairn Island? It just so happened that there was a marine proctor in Detroit by the name of Sparky Meadows. I knew him through mutual friends in Detroit, and he arranged for a company to take these materials to Pitcairn Island for free. About six months later, through the arrangements made by the Shaw-Sevill Albion Shipping Company of London, the materials arrived, packaged in huge crates made by a Traverse City lumber company.

The islanders took these crates and filled them up with curios: wood carvings, and flying fish, or turtles made from miro wood gathered from Henderson Island, prints, stamps, placemats, and other items, and sent them to Traverse City.

We had a sale here at WTCM, and many people in Traverse City bought curios from Pitcairn, and they have them to this day. One of the great collector's items was a basket made of dyed reeds with the words "Pitcairn Island" on the side. These baskets sold very fast and are valued, I know, by people in the city today.

A good deal of money was raised by this sale, and that in itself created another problem. How could I send the cash by mail? I called the postmaster of the United States and asked how I could send money to Pitcairn Island, and he arranged for me to send it through the postmaster of Panama. We wrapped and rewrapped this bundle, $1,200 in cash, and sent it to the postmaster in Colon. We didn't hear, and we didn't hear. Finally, after eighteen months Parkin Christian, the present council head, wrote to say the money had arrived. It had been crossing and recrossing the ocean and couldn't be delivered until recently because of storms.

Parkin Christian came to the United States a while after this, and he stayed a week at my home in Traverse City. It was in Traverse that he celebrated his eighty-fourth birthday. He was being sent around the country by the Seventh Day Adventist Church, which is very active on Pitcairn Island; but I sponsored him a bit too. I took him to Chicago, where he appeared on a program on WGN and made quite a hit. Then I took him to Washington, D.C., where I decided to have a little luncheon for him. I called a few members of the FCC and one or two congressmen and asked them to come over for lunch to meet the head man from Pitcairn Island. I said they could bring a friend or two if they wished.

When the time came for the luncheon, I had over a hundred guests. We moved out of one dining room into another, then another, to hold all the people who had come to meet the guy from Pitcairn Island.

We went on to New York, where I wanted Mr. Christian to meet Wally Watt, the man who had helped bring ham radio to Pitcairn Island. As we got off the elevator to go see Mr. Watt, who should we see but David Sarnoff of RCA? I introduced David to Mr. Christian, and David remarked on Mr. Christian's height, six feet six or seven. Then he added, "You know I was on Pitcairn Island myself once."

"I know," said Mr. Christian, and then went on to remind Mr. Sarnoff that he had been the coxswain of a boat that had rowed Mr. Sarnoff to the island during an emergency situation. Mr. Sarnoff had been a passenger on a yacht, I think it was the Hearst yacht, that was cruising past Pitcairn when a distress call came. Mrs. McCoy, an inhabitant on the island, had acute appendicitis, and it was necessary to remove her appendix. Nobody on the island could do that, so they were radioing for help. The yacht had a surgeon aboard, and when he went ashore to perform the operation on Mrs. McCoy, David Sarnoff went with him.

"How did you remember me after thirty or forty years?" David asked Mr. Christian.

"We don't have many visitors on Pitcairn Island, and I think I must remember every one," the old man had smiled.

I still haven't been to Pitcairn Island, but one of the things I want to do before I close my life is to set foot on that small, but warmly friendly and interesting spot way out there in the Pacific.

Although I didn't get to Pitcairn Island during this time, a couple of other dreams did come together for me during the Sixties. The first was the farm I had dreamed for several years of owning in the beautiful Grand Traverse region.

I began looking at property and settled on a remote but lovely farm in Wexford County, which had been owned by a family named Sobert. The little farm house stood just as it was back in 1900, with the house heated by a wood-burning parlor stove. In the kitchen was a tremendous wood-burning range able to cook any amount of coffee or hot cakes. The electric pump was fed from an old well under the former windmill. As I explored the property, I found such interesting items as a hallrack, a grain cradle, a sleigh, and an old carriage. A china cabinet there reminded me of ones my relatives had years ago in Philly. I drove around the fields, which had seen a lot of farming in the hundred years since the immigrant Soberts had come to northern Michigan to begin a new life. There was no telephone, and a mile-long lane with pine trees on either side led to the farm house. It was just right; I bought it in the early part of the Sixties.

The family, but particularly I, began spending time at the farm. Being away from that ringing phone was just what I needed as the demands on my time at the station grew and all the extracurricular activities started demanding more time—too much time, I was beginning to sometimes think. At Soberts' nobody could reach me; for all practical purposes, I didn't exist, at least for a while.

One of my favorite "haunts" was the cemetery. Immigrant families buried their dead in the little Down Cemetery near the Soberts' property, and a look at the gravestones can reveal a history of Americanization for a family like the Soberts. Sopeslab, Soperslav, Soberslav, Sobert. This is the way in which the names gradually changed.

I looked at the patent and saw it was signed by President Ulysses S. Grant. This was probably the signature of a scribe, but the name was there all right. I began to be very much aware of the history of the region, and as I visited the Soberts' house, I thought about what it must have been like to have been an immigrant.

Following the Civil War, the Michigan area started to develop rapidly. People were coming to claim war land grants made available to veterans; the widows of veterans were coming to get these compensation grants, then selling them to immigrants, the future homesteaders of America. Many of these widows worked through "People's Agents." These were businessmen who put the interested parties in touch with immigrants coming from Europe, so that they might sell their land.

At that time there was a great out-migration from eastern Europe. Russians, Poles, Bohemians, Slavs, Serbs, and others were coming to the "Land of Opportunity" and fleeing confusion, war, and oppression in their own lands.

Those coming, like the Soberts, to northern Michigan had a tremendous trip with lots of hardships, and it certainly must have taken perserverance to finish the trip. Many of the Bohemians who came to northern Michigan sailed across the ocean on sailing ships as steerage passengers. Even before they got on the ship, they made long journeys through eastern Europe to reach the seaport from which they had departed.

Most arrived in New York. Here they were in the dreamed-of Utopia, but where were they really? Many took the small steamboats up the Hudson to Troy, a full day's journey. At Troy they boarded mule-drawn canal boats for a three-week journey all the way across New York State to Buffalo, New York. Then at Buffalo, they would board a sailing schooner for a week's trip across the Great Lakes. Those in the northern Michigan area usually landed at Leland, which at that time was an important Great Lakes port. Taking the stage from the dock at Leland, they went overland a mile or two to a landing at Lake Leelanau (then called Carp Lake) where they boarded a small steamer to go to Perrins Landing, or Bingham, and finally took a stage or train to Traverse to complete their journey.

In Traverse they would have to outfit themselves to survive until the land they had bought would yield a cash crop. Hannah, Lay Mercantile was the great outfitting company for these arriving immigrants. Here they made arrangements for their needed supplies. Some would purchase mule teams, others teams of oxen, or perhaps even horses. They would acquire a rough wagon, manufactured in Traverse City by the Petertyl Wagon Works; and they would load in the hard rations, tools, and their families, and start inland looking for that particular piece of property described in the land patent they now had. So the Soberts would have come on out and constructed some sort of temporary shelter. Some people excavated caves in the sides of banks to provide their first shelter. Others constructed crude cabins like the one which I imagined stood on the Sobert property, judging from descriptions on other property grants.

At the time that people like the Soberts were arriving, about 1870 or so, the land was still heavily timbered, and the sawmill operations in the Traverse area were going full blast. The first cash crops of these newcomers who made this country what it is, was the log crop, which was sold to an entrepreneur like Gibbs Brothers or Perry Hannah. Many of the old land descriptions show the paper work on the sale of timber to these lumber barons, who made fortunes in the sawmill business. It wasn't until about the tenth year that these new Americans could hope to raise agricultural crops in a profitable enough way to live. In the meantime, they sold their timber, and little by little, cleared enough land to raise their staple crops such as corn, wheat, and the many truck-garden items the family would need.

These pioneers raised at least one cow, for milk only, and some pigs and chickens. The hardworking wives made necessary household money by selling cabbage, lettuce, and potatoes from their truck gardens, plus their eggs, homemade butter, and other attractive farm produce. Most of the rural people in those days ate pork, chicken, and game, not beef. Soberts reflected all these pioneer habits. Standing on the sacred eighty acres was the little farm house, a chicken house, a granary, and a pig house. The old barn was torn down a few years ago and the materials used to construct a fine two-car garage. The windmill was taken down, but all of the materials were saved and stored in the outbuildings.

The children, of course, walked to school; and a mile or two was the normal trip. The school houses were all one-room and were spaced at about three mile intervals, so that about a mile and a half would be the maximum walk. This helped make good farmers out of the kids and strengthened their legs.

The schoolteachers in those days didn't have all the degrees that are required nowadays, but they had something that was perhaps more important. They were nearly all neighborhood girls, and they knew the children from the time they were born. These teachers weren't paid much, but they sure were dedicated. They taught in schoolhouses that had been built by their neighbors. It wasn't even necessary to buy lumber up here; the neighbors simply cut logs and hauled them to the mill, and the lumber resulting from the logs would go half to the sawmill operator and half to the owner of the logs. Then they would take this lumber and construct a schoolhouse for their youngsters. Around the Sobert farm and all over northern Michigan and the Midwest are these small schoolhouses where an entire generation was taught patriotism, the basic fundamentals of reading and writing and math and a positive attitude towards hard work.

The property papers for the Soberts' included many strange documents. For instance, there were the discharged mortgage papers for $800 from the National Bank of Wexford. The mention of that bank in Wexford brings another ghost out of the past.

Wexford in the 1870's was a prosperous little village with a bank, its quota of saloons and churches, many comfortable homes, and other signs of civilization. In the Seventies the railroad was constructed northward from Grand Rapids up to Traverse City and the Straits of Mackinac. There was more wheeling and dealing in this process than you can imagine, and one of the places dealt out was the thriving little village of Wexford. In spite of all its advantages as a town, Wexford had no electricity as yet; and this, along with a bunch of political considerations, spelled its doom. The railroad did not go through Wexford, but instead through a smaller town known as Buckley.

This was the finish of Wexford. The twenty-four room hotel had no guests, while the eight-room hotel at Buckley was filled all the time. The taverns and saloons in Buckley enjoyed a good business, with several trains per day stopping there; and the saloons in Wexford went broke. Soon Buckley became the center of banking, had a feed store and grain mill and all of the other community things the surrounding farm people needed; and then Wexford died.

I visited Wexford's site out of curiosity and found a thick, concrete box which was the bank vault of the National Bank of Wexford, which had furnished the Soberts' mortgage money. Looking around at the intersection, I saw hay fields with stone and concrete steps right in the field, all that is left of businesses or proud homes. In the center of the town site, these miscellaneous pieces of civilization's flotsam are all over the place. The grazing cows do not seem to mind that they are stepping around the ruins of a decayed town.

At this farm, in the middle of this piece of Traverse City area history, I found a lot of contentment and peace. I also used the Soberts' farm (as I continued to call it, even though I now owned it) for meetings involving Traverse City community activities. I would go to Jerry Oleson's market, buy some steaks and potato salad and cold drinks, call up a committee or group I was working with, and take them down that winding lane to the farm house. There we would grill outside, drink beer, and plan whatever it was that needed planning in a congenial, pleasant atmosphere. More work always seemed to get done that way.

In 1968 I found Soberts' was the perfect place to plan what was one of the biggest undertakings I had been involved with in Traverse City's growth—the Great Lakes Maritime Academy. It, too, was a sort of dream of mine—for the college.

Back in 1957, I began to go a little boat-crazy in terms of Northwestern Michigan College. A professor was trying to get a dozen or so students to make a European tour. As I thought about it, I began to wonder if it would be possible to get 500 students or so on a big ship and take them all on a tour. We could hold classes every day on the ship, with every student taking a job assignment of some kind. We could make about ten stops in a college quarter of ten weeks. If the cost could be kept down to roughly the cost of a college quarter, we could make this floating university available to thousands of students otherwise deprived of knowing what being on a ship was like.

I travelled, looked at ships, talked to people, visited shipping companies, and in the process met Admiral John "Dutch" Will. At that time Admiral Will headed the Military Sea Transportation Service. He was operating a whole fleet of transports and encouraged me with my "Floating University" project.

He opened many doors and presented a good deal of information, but in the final stages of getting this thing off the ground, the college said "no," and the idea folded. What didn't fold was my enthusiasm for having the college involved in some type of maritime venture. It was natural, with our location on Lake Michigan.

The idea surfaced again, this time with real feasibility, when Senator Bob Griffin sent us a letter saying that the government had Federal aid for projects such as maritime academies. There were already five academies, all on the seacoasts, but there was none on the important Great Lakes shipping system. The college had, meantime, expressed interest in some type of maritime training venture, which it voiced through its Board of Trustees in 1962, and a lot of people in the area thought it would be a great idea to train young people right here in Traverse City for careers in Great Lakes shipping.

So the question in 1968 was what to do, how to do it, and who would be involved. It was an ideal job to take care of at Soberts'. The trustees were invited for dinner at the farm, along with Arnell Engstrom and Ken Thompson.

Arnell Engstrom, as you will recall, was that representative who was also a founder of the college. He had been by this time named by the Board of Trustees as a "Fellow of the College," the highest honor the school could confer. Ken Thompson was my attorney. Formerly an official of Chrysler in their legal department, he had moved to Traverse City like many people, for a fuller life. He was a supporter of the college and had been a law partner of Bob Griffin, and his opinions, we thought, would be valuable as we talked about a Maritime Academy.

Everyone had too much to eat, and when the table was cleared we moved into the little dining room with the curved china closet in the corner and the round oak table, for our business meeting. The letter from Senator Griffin was read. Andy Olson opened up right away with, "Let's get going," backed up by just about everybody. The Board of Trustees and Director Preston Tanis were unanimous in their opinion that the venture was worth pursuing; and the chairman (myself) was instructed to pursue this venture and see what could be done.

I'd like to reconstruct the membership of the board, because it shows not only the enthusiasm of the group at that particular time for a maritime venture, but also the quality of leadership that the college attracted and the experience that came out of that in the Sixties.

Dr. Warren Cline was an especially interesting fellow. He was (and is) an M. D. in private practice, specializing in cardiology. He was first trained as a scientist, then took up the study of medicine. He was a pursuit pilot during World War II, and his knowledge of technical subjects was tremendous. He was involved in establishing the college's first school of nursing, and was always associated with that program after that.

Jim Beckett was the local manager of Michigan Bell Telephone. He was intensely interested in the college and has always been involved in the town's civic growth. Dr. Harry Weitz was chief Roentgenologist at the Munson Medical Center. He was a long-time rag sailor with his own private craft and was especially interested in our moving with the college into the maritime training area.

Then there was Julius Sleder, ex-Navy man in the Big War(II) and also the local Ford, Lincoln and Mercury dealer; Jerry McCarthy, a graduate of the Naval Academy at Annapolis; and Andy Olson, the local 4-H Club agent for several counties and founder of the Twin Lakes 4-H Camp.

So the Board made a decision to go for the academy, and Senator Griffin was informed. He suggested a trip to Washington where he would meet with the Coast Guard, Navy, and other interested parties. We planned the meeting between Christmas and New Year's, but the weather refused to cooperate; and the meeting had to be postponed, because all the airports in the East were closed down. But the lads in Washington did not let our town down. They made arrangements for all of the Washington people to board an airplane and fly to Traverse City. It was quite a meeting—involved were Governor William Milliken; Herb DeJong, state Secretary of Commerce; state Senator Jack Toepp; Representative Engstrom; Senator Griffin; Sid Wolner of Senator Hart's office; an executive assistant to Congressman Guy Vander Jagt; Admiral William Rae, Commandant of the Ninth Coast Guard District of the U.S.; Admiral Hirschfield, President of the Lake Carriers' Association; Captain Reed of the U.S. Coast Guard Headquarters in Washington; and several representatives of the United States Navy.

They met with Thompson and the board of Trustees of the college at the "Top" of the Park Place Motor Inn. Ted Okerstrom, the manager of the Park Place, served what has got to be the most sumptuous luncheon ever seen in Traverse, and the visitors could plainly see that the town meant business and was pulling out all the stops to get an academy here.

The local people and their government representatives, of course, backed the proposal. Captain Reed of the Coast Guard, and the Maritime Administration people took a dim view of the project, pointing out the high costs and other problems. They particularly pointed to increasing automation in the maritime industry. Fewer, not more sailors, would be needed, they seemed to be saying.

I took the floor as chairman of the Board, and I realized I was going to have to oppose that viewpoint pretty strongly, if we were going to get this job done. I, like the rest of the college Board, believed that there was a great future for an academy, and that statistics pointed to the need for more officers on the Great Lakes, not fewer. This was at considerable variance with the official speakers; but Admiral Hirschfield, President of the Carriers' Association, did back me up.

Well, we had tried to do our homework, and what we had found out was this:

(1) At that time the typical officer working on the Great Lakes was ten years older than he should have been under the new retirement programs.

(2) There was a serious shortage of pilots in the Detroit River, the St. Clair River, in the lock systems of the St. Lawrence, and even in the Welland Canal.

(3) Congress was just then in the process of extending the licensing requirements for auxiliary vessels so that men on tugs, motorized barges, and other craft would have to be licensed. This would open up thousands of additional jobs on the waterways.

I spoke about these things and suggested we tour the facilities at the college. When we did this, the officials from the Coast Guard and Navy were surprised to find that the college had about fifty percent of the available classes already in operation and that it had deep-water dockage available with very little cost. I know they were surprised at the amount of research we had done, and when they left at about 3:30 on the plane, their impression was much different than on arrival.

We had a great deal of confidence in what we could do if only given the chance, and a trip to one of the other academies only confirmed our belief in Traverse City's ability to set up a first-class academy. Art Moenkhaus and I travelled to Galveston to see the Texas State Maritime Academy, which was the smallest and newest at that time. It had been in existence six years. There really wasn't much to see. At that time this academy consisted of one ship provided by the Federal government and an academic program operated by Texas A&M some 200 miles distant. There was no small boat program; and the only dock facility available was the leased berthing space for the ship, which during the visit was in Norwegian waters. We were glad to see this program, because it gave us the courage of our convictions about what the college could do.

I began thinking about a site, and almost at once an opportunity developed, although I had to proceed very quietly and tactfully at this point. In the first place, the Board of

Trustees had only committed themselves to investigate the possibilities of a maritime academy, and talk about a site would have been at that point premature. Much more data and design work really did need to be done. In the second place, Traverse City is a grapevine town; we didn't want the maritime academy to become a cocktail party conversation topic before it was even off the drawing board. So I proceeded slowly.

Actually, the first talks about what became the site of the maritime academy developed almost by accident, at least casually. I had several lunches with Wynn Klotzback, the president of Cherry Growers, Incorporated about some problems connected with the cherry industry at that time; and I made some suggestions about marketing cherries for the consumer market. As we talked, I told him about the college's hopes of having an academy in a good location in Traverse City. I told him I thought that his own plant would make an ideal site, although I did not see how it could be made available to us. It was located on the main street of Traverse City and contained about 600 feet of waterfront, partially developed with sheet piling. This site had eleven acres and was about halfway between the main college campus and the center of Traverse City.

About a month later Wynn called to say he had done a rough economic estimate of Cherry Growers' situation and thought a new plant and location might be a good thing for them. The company had owned a site near Grawn for several years, and they were aware that being all on one floor in a new location would reduce their operating costs considerably. Also, they admitted that there was a pollution problem in the Bay at the present location; in a new spot they could construct a lagoon for sewage disposal.

Still, neither of us was involving our boards; it was all too preliminary. At the end of discussions, and with Ken Thompson acting as attorney of record for college, it was agreed that the college could make a tender of $300,000 for the property, creating a trust that would purchase an additional portion for the sum of $50,000, making the entire project a $350,000 proposition. Now I could go to the Board of Trustees of Northwestern Michigan College.

The board just couldn't believe that this valuable shorefront property could be had for such a sum and readily granted the proposition. The property contained in excess of 100,000 square feet of floor space in addition to eleven acres of land. The floor space could be converted in many ways to exactly the kind of facility the college needed for expansion—a technical center for the instruction of machine shop, automotive shop, and electronics. We could open a computer center and develop a printing program.

We incorporated the Northwestern Michigan College Foundation, which would purchase a part of the property at the same time as the college made its purchase for the technical center. Renting out warehouse space in the unoccupied buildings would provide money to maintain the property and pay interest on a $50,000 loan. Trustees for the new foundation were myself, Jake Beers of the Traverse City State Bank; and Will Munnecke of Leland, the former general manager of the *Chicago Sun-Times* and a long-time friend of the college. Ken Thompson was appointed secretary of the foundation. In one year's time about $15,000 of the principle on the loan had been paid off, and the interest was up to date. In addition many repairs to the facility were paid for.

The $300,000 that the college put up for their portion of the project came from $150,000 in local tax funds and $150,000 from state matching funds. Immediately the college entered into a major program of remodelling; and of the $180,000 involved in this renovation, the state of Michigan provided $90,000, and $90,000 came from local tax money.

Cherry Growers benefitted from their new plant; they merged with Duffy Mott, which had a tremendous product line to go with the Cherry Growers productions; and subsequently Duffy Mott merged with U.S. Tobacco. Traverse City thus became the headquarters of a division of one of the largest consumer-product companies in the world.

As soon as word got out to the town, the local do-gooders and what would be called today "environmentalists" began to badger me. The college should tear down those buildings, plant trees, and make it a park instead of developing it as a maritime academy and technical center. The odd part about all this was that most of these people were exactly the same ones who were supporting the power plant now being constructed on a prime lot a mile from the new academy building. Here's the story of the power plant rhubarb. The city owned a site of beautiful lake frontage, about 600 feet of it. Next to it was another site they owned, which had some warehouse buildings on it that they planned to make into a park. Instead of building elsewhere and using that first 600 feet of space to make a large park, they built what most people considered to be a giant eyesore of a power plant right on Grandview Parkway. Then many of these same people who backed the power plant came to me, protesting the college's use of a lot obviously best used for industrial purposes. Strange how the human mind works.

Meanwhile, people were coming to us with strong backing for the academy. I met Don Goosetrey, a graduate of the National Maritime Academy of Kings Point, New York; and he introduced me to a friend who worked for the Commerce Department of the State of Michigan, which was in charge of maritime activities. This friend, Joe Cook, came and toured our facilities and enthusiastically backed the plan. With him on that touring visit had come Mike Hemmick, who soon turned out to be our first professional consultant and a real asset. Soon the Board of Trustees of the college met to offer Mike the position of consultant, with the goal of acquiring a ship for the proposed Great Lakes Maritime Academy. He accepted.

Captain Reed of the United States Coast Guard invited me to go with him on an official visit to the Maine Maritime Academy. I flew to Bucksport, Maine, and met the captain at the Old Inn. What atmosphere! Maine is the Lobster State, and did they know how to serve delicious lobster! The next morning we had a tour from Lieutenant Commander Gott, who was soon to be leaving for another assignment. His chest stuck out when he pointed out that Governor Curtis, then Governor of Maine, was a graduate of the State of Maine Maritime Academy.

Their training ship, the *State of Maine*, was a great public relations tool for the state. It carried an exhibit in cooperation with the state Chamber of Commerce, showing the agricultural and manufacturing products and natural resources of the state. The ship visited foreign countries and invited local officials to have dinner on board and take a tour of the ship. I also was impressed with the new physical education center and the activities building at the academy which housed all of the eating and recreation facilities.

While I was there, we kicked around at length the idea of a training ship. The other five academies had boats which wouldn't suit us; they were all large passenger ships of about 18,000 to 20,000 tons burden, and they were expensive to operate. What we were envisioning was a ship that would carry about eighty cadets and would be low-cost and seaworthy in the Great Lakes waters. Commander Gott made the suggestion that perhaps we might consider a type of boat which had recently visited the academy—it was called an ATA. It was a World War II, 1,500 horsepower boat, 143 feet in length and equipped with a crew of forty-four men and nine officers. This turned out to be a very lucky suggestion indeed.

I returned home after a tour of the beautiful seacoast of Maine, and the more I thought about it, the more an ATA sounded like it could be the ideal ship for the new academy. A call to the U.S. Navy Bureau of Ships eventually uncovered the fact that there was an ATA, ideal for our purposes, named the *Allegheny* which was on special assignment with the Hudson Research Laboratories, a division of Columbia University, for oceanographic research. The program under which it operated was about to end, and the disposition of the ship wasn't certain.

Senator Griffin's office got to work and came back with a report that the standard procedures would be time-consuming and possibly dangerous to our cause. Acquiring a ship like the *Allegheny* would mean going through government channels—Departments of Health, Education and Welfare, as well as the U.S. Navy, the Secretary of Defense, the Defense Supply Agency, and the General Services Administration. All of the bureaucrats would have an opportunity, before the boat would ever come to us, to strip it of whatever their department wanted—we could see one agency wanting the radar, another the radio gear, another the gyrocompass. We decided to work to bypass the standard procedure if it was at all possible.

I found out there was an ATA, a sister to the *Allegheny* named the *Accokeek*, in the Philadelphia Navy Yard. I went to visit it, and it seemed just right for our use. Then the skipper of the *Accokeek* told me he believed the *Allegheny* was going into mothballs, now that her mission for the Hudson Research Lab was completed. That did it. Now the race to acquire the *Allegheny* became official.

The Navy would not indicate where the *Allegheny* was, but they did tell us that several important modifications had been made on her when she was doing oceanographic duty. It was at this point that we involved my old friend Admiral John Will, who later became the chairman of the Board of American Export-Isbrandsen Lines. John agreed to help, and finally correct information began to come in.

The *Allegheny* was presently tied up at the MSTS dock terminal at Bayonne, New Jersey, and the captain had already been contacted and would welcome a visit to the ship, according to Admiral Will. Mike Hemmick was called, and we made arrangements to view that ship. It's hard to describe my feelings when we got into that tremendous marine terminal at Bayonne. We walked all over the pier looking for the *Allegheny* and when I caught my first sight of her, my heart jumped. Was she ever beautiful. Just exactly what the new academy was looking for.

After proper introductions, we went aboard; and we stayed aboard for about six hours, visiting every nook and cranny. There, right off the beam of the ship stood that grand old lady, the Statue of Liberty; just past her, the lights of New

York. On an adjacent pier were a number of ships tied up in storage; and the ferry boats, tankers, and all kinds of other vessels were steaming by, but our interests were all with our ship. If there was any doubt about the use of the ship for the basic training in the academy, it was dispelled in the first half hour. She was in fine shape, and any modifications were all to the good.

The next day we inspected ever further (Mike Hemmick donning dungarees), and we saw the salvage hold, the chain locker, the tank bilges, and the general stowage areas. The engineering officer started the big diesels, and they purred like a kitten. Surely a trip to Washington was in order, and I went there almost immediately with Don Goosetrey. Mr. Sol Elson of HEW gave us a briefing on general procedures and took us to the Pentagon to see Captain Paul Hannon. He urged us to take a different ship that was already in mothballs; we could drive it away that very afternoon, he said, if we wished. There were, of course, reasons why we couldn't do that. Those ships in mothballs had been pillaged for parts, and about half of them had wooden hulls; freezing in the Great Lakes would wreck them. No, we said, the *Allegheny* was our ship.

Captain Hannon disagreed and took a very conservative stance, as he should have done. Too many people with projects get so carried away with their dreams and ideas that they lose sight of reality. He represented the Navy; it's the job of people in his position to keep that from happening. We felt that we had reality actually working on our side, however. If the Navy wanted to keep the *Allegheny*, they would have to expend considerable time and money unmodifying her, removing an extra deck house and doing numerous modifications, to prepare her for mothballs. It was a slightly unusual situation, and we thought it had to work in our favor.

We had dinner that night with Senator Bob Griffin and his wife. The senator had just led the floor fight to oppose confirmation of Judge Abe Fortas to the Supreme Court, and we spent a pleasant dinner hour talking about that Fortas battle and the battle to get *Allegheny.* The folks with me were impressed by the fact that the senator was just as down-to-earth as the guy next door. He wasn't impressed with his new position; it was just like old times back when he was a lawyer in Traverse City and we were discussing the establishment of a local college.

On the way home, we stopped by Governor Milliken's office and received some encouragement for the project, along with caution and concern over the financing at the state level. Still, the Legislature was already at work on an authorization bill, and it would not be long before it was actually passed.

It seemed as if it would be almost impossible to wrench that ship away from the United States Navy. We had felt this when we arrived at Bayonne and Lieutenant (JG) Doug Burris had almost not wanted to let us come on board. I had explained about what we had in mind, and Burris's answer was typical of what the entire Navy thought. He said, "The Navy doesn't give ships away; besides you're a bunch of amateurs. How will you sail her home to Traverse City? You can't handle this thing in the Atlantic in the winter. Man, you just don't understand." Still, within a month, and in a way that still makes my head spin, the *Allegheny* was ours.

I don't remember all of the people we talked to in Lansing, or Washington, or any of the other places; I only know many of us were on the phone hour after hour; and with the help of Joe Cook in the Department of Commerce, Pete Holmes in Senator Griffin's office, Senator Hart, Congressman Guy Vander Jagt, Phil Ruppe, and even future President Jerry Ford, Washington finally took action. The *Allegheny* would be decommissioned and given to Northwestern Michigan College in Traverse City, Michigan. Just about a month from the time that I had been reluctantly welcomed aboard by a bewildered Lieutenant Burris, I was handed the ship's nameplate by this same lieutenant. Navy Tug 195 belonged free and clear to NMC of Traverse City.

CHAPTER SEVEN

BRINGING THE *ALLEGHENY* HOME

Now we were faced with the pleasant but challenging job of bringing our training ship for the Great Lakes Maritime Academy back to Traverse City, and the job became one for the entire town to tackle. We circulated word that we would be needing a crew, and within a few days forty people had signed up. Naturally Mike Hemmick, whose last command had been a Viet Nam ammunition boat, was captain. He would be assisted by such Traverse Bay sailors as Greg Fiebing, an ex-Navy man on active duty until 1961; Charles "Bo" Bosardet, an aircraft skipper; and Bill Thomas, who owned Thomas's Coffee Shop, and would help in the galley.

Meanwhile, in the Navy Yard, the many complicated things that are necessary to declassify a ship were underway. The ship had to be admeasured (measured) inside and out to produce an official document, and a reinspection had to occur to insure that the boat was safe. All fire fighting systems had to be checked and the voyage and crew requirements analyzed. All this we had been busy arranging even before we had the final, official word from the Navy that we did have the ship. (The Department of the Interior was trying, up to the very last, to grab it from us before the college could get official title.)

Finally, word had come from Senator Griffin's office that the college would be given official title to the *Allegheny*, and that the navy would even throw in a ceremony to show their good will.

It was November, 1969, and I think it was one of the proudest days of my life. It was some twelve years in arriving, and I had so much of a feeling of thrill that it was hard to do the necessary things. We went to the *Allegheny* and found about twenty guest chairs set up for the decommissioning ceremony. Quite a few guests came on board. There were several officers representing the Philadelphia Navy Yard, including Admiral Veth; there was Captain Walter Chadwick, representing the Navy's Auxiliary Fleet; and Captain Joe Kennedy of the *Allegheny*; along with Doug Burris; and there were representatives of Senator Griffin, Congressmen Ruppe and Vander Jagt; people from the Department of Commerce; Warren Cline of the college's Board of Trustees—even Ishmael, the ship's dog, was present.

The ceremony was brief and at times so moving that I found myself with tears in my eyes. A Navy Chaplain thanked God for the safety of the various members of the crew of the *Allegheny* during the time it was doing its work for its country. Captain Chadwick said, "Speaking on behalf of the Atlantic Fleet to which *Allegheny* was assigned—its future is heartening. It will be welcomed by people interested in the life of a ship; and we trust the new owners will get as good use from her as the Navy has."

I replied, saying Northwestern Michigan College would "give her a good ride." Then the Union Jack and the Stars and Stripes were hauled down, and the boat's commissioning ribbon turned over to Lieutenant Kennedy. From that moment, the ship was retired.

Word of all this was in Traverse almost within minutes; I called the station and had a radio broadcast direct, and a lot of the guests spoke live on the air. This was when people in Traverse really began to be excited. It didn't look like it would be long before we could begin to move the ship to its new home in the Bay. I had an editorial on the station, telling about the decommissioning of the boat, saying that we had taken the three television sets on board over to the Philadelphia Naval Hospital, installing them for the amputees who were Viet Nam veterans. I mentioned that it sure would be nice if we could do something for these fine Americans, perhaps even if it were only making them a batch of home-made fudge.

To my surprise, my remarks, made really as an afterthought and because I had been sincerely saddened when I had visited that hospital, inspired by the courage I had seen, became an idea the town took hold of right away. Both the radio announcers and the public in Traverse City dubbed February 20, 1960 as "Fudge Day." The *Record Eagle* supported "Fudge Day," too, and hundreds of people began making fudge. I had the idea of asking everybody who made fudge to enclose a letter to a G.I., aimed at cheering him up. Gifts should be wrapped, the hospital suggested, and we would need some 600 to 800 gifts, quite a few. Some people didn't know how to make fudge, but said they would try peanut brittle. We agreed to add cherry pie to the offerings, in honor of our city's crop and Washington's Birthday and the Tri-County Medical Auxiliary added 800 packages of toasted, salted pecans.

Fudge Day, February 20. A few packages came in, and we put them on the desk. By 9:00 A.M. there were more than 200 packages at the station, and it was necessary to start piling them on the floor. By noon the count was over 500, and it was impossible to keep track of the quantity. At 5:00 the entire office staff packaged the gifts, and the count totalled 1,468 packages by the time it was all through.

In caravan several of us, including my wife Anne, took the

packages to Philadelphia, going also to make preparations for the crew that would deliver the *Allegheny* to Traverse City.

Much work had been done in the period since decommissioning. The ship had been painted—75 gallons for the exterior—she had been moved to a rented berth because of some complications and misunderstandings in the Navy Yard, and she had been admeasured and certified. Now the electricity was ready to be turned on to get the auxiliary engines running and to just generally light up the ship.

Andy Olson was our first cook, and he had come as a part of the fudge caravan. Now he was poking around in the galley, pleased with the sight of a large galley and decent equipment. He was as happy as a bug in a rug.

We brought one ton of dry stores from our two station wagons and stowed them, temporarily, in the ship's lab, awaiting the regular crew's arrival so they could be put where they belonged. Captain Mike Hemmick was testing the engines and readying all. Finally he locked up the ship. The next time we unlocked the ship, we would take it 3,500 miles home, three weeks hence.

An important job was left, however, before we could leave Philadelphia. Monday morning, February 24, we went looking for the Philadelphia Naval Hospital.

When Lieutenant Holiday and Miss Tina of the Hospital were informed that downstairs there was the Thomas Restaurant van loaded with some two tons of fudge wrapped up in gift wrapping, along with many other goodies, and that someone was asking where should they be unloaded, they almost fainted. They arranged for the gifts to be taken to the amputees immediately.

It was especially interesting that all of the news agencies had been informed, and they all promised to cover the event. None showed up for the occasion; and the people at the hospital were not the least surprised, as this had been the case many times over. It appears that all of these 1,000 wounded that lay in the Philadelphia Naval Hospital were not very interesting to the news people. This was a big crowd of integrated young Americans, for the most part under twenty years of age, minus legs and arms, hoping for some kind of rehabilitation and awfully happy they could come back on a bed instead of in a pine box, but the press was too busy to pay attention to them.

Our Cherry Queen who accompanied us was just wonderful. You could plainly see that she was affected by all of these shot-up young men of her own age, but she was a brave girl. She went to every one of those men, black and white, and presented them with a gift from the people of Traverse City, and these men also did a job of reacting. One boy from Kentucky said, as he read an attached letter, "These people never heard of me, yet look at what they did."

One young man was covered up with a quilt of many colors. He lay perfectly still, and it was plain to see that he had no legs at all. The nurse said, "We are going to lose that boy—he has no will to live." He was shot-up just a week before and was white as a sheet. He hadn't spoken a word since arriving at this hospital. The Queen went over to him and looked at his face, and he turned his head away. Then she leaned over and kissed his forehead, and he slowly turned his head towards her and said a few words. In almost nothing flat they were conversing, and the nurse said, "Just look at that." The Queen left him a beautiful package.

Much later, as we were getting ready to leave the hospital, getting our coats and hats from the outer office of the Captain in charge of the hospital, that captain came out of his office. He came right over to Julie Ann and said, "I hear that young man has been propped up and is asking for something to eat. You might have saved that boy's life and I'm grateful." This really shook up our gal from Traverse.

The little favors done for these fine men who made such a tremendous sacrifice for our country were really appreciated, we could tell. It is depressing to realize that at that time 200,000 men had been wounded in the Viet Nam War and some 60,000 were hospitalized yet; and the public took little notice. Many people were driving their fine cars down Pattison Avenue in front of the Veterans Hospital in Philadelphia, seemingly taking no account of what was going on inside. With feelings of mixed accomplishment and sadness we returned to Traverse.

* * * *

On March 15 we had returned to Philly and were excitedly awaiting the arrival of the crew from Traverse City who would take *Allegheny* home. Soon they came, by car or plane—Andy Olson, Bo Bosardet; Mr. Turdahl, the chief licensed engineer; Greg Fiebing, Bill Thomas, Bob Rufli, Russ Jacobus, Paul Jones, Jim Stevens, Bob Cummins, Dave Yeomans, Dr. Adam McClay, Dr. Bill Petersen, and Dr. Warren Cline and others. Don Goosetrey was also with us; he was returning to Traverse City to make arrangements for dockage and St. Lawrence passage for the ship. Russ Jacobus worked as many as twenty-one hours a day to get the *Allegheny* ready for the Coast Guard inspection on Saturday. There were more broken pipe fittings, frozen controls and other deficiencies than you can believe. He was up in the middle of the night watching the boiler, making adjustments to the auxiliary engine that was supplying the power, and fixing steam lines that broke. All we heard for several days was, "We can never be ready by Saturday," spoken in a sort of frog-like voice. Russ had contracted laryngitis through long hours and hard work. Still, when Friday came, there was Russ saying, "She'll be ready to sail as soon as we take water aboard." That job never seemed to end. At 2:00 P.M. he started filling up tanks, and he still wasn't done at 8:00 P.M. Friday afternoon we were swamped with forty media people—newspaper, radio/TV; they swarmed all over the ship, shooting movie film for TV, interviewing, taking still pictures, and kind of getting in the way of operation.

Finally, Saturday dawned; and after a lengthy Coast Guard inspection and a million minor delays, we were cleared to leave at 8:00 A.M. the next morning. Saturday night late all was done, the watch set, the captain ashore, crew bedded down for the big day: departure from Philadelphia, my childhood city, with my big dream of having a ship for the college realized.

Sailing day, oh, happy sailing day! By 7:00 everyone had been assigned formal watches and job assignments and had chowed down and was aware this was not a pleasure boat ride, but a working experience on a working ship. They were an amateur crew, although many had some good credentials and had passed a Coast Guard "course" and had gotten a license (not much of anything, really, but they were certified to go), and now they would have to learn how to sail a Navy tug through the Atlantic in the winter, as Lieutenant Burris had said, by on-the-job training, mostly. I had great faith in them all, really, but there was an edge of apprehension connected with it, if only because of the unpredictability of the weather and the awe in which I held the ocean. With three doctors on board we were not too worried about medical problems, but some of these lads were wondering what was going to happen to them as this ship rounded Cape May and the swell began. We heard it had been blowing for nearly six weeks, and no fishing boats had operated out of Cape May. When it blows for such a long time, it takes a long time to settle down.

Well, we cast off anyway, with Dr. Warren Cline on telegraph watch, and Bob Rufli on the wheel, Captain Mike on the bridge, and a pilot, and an apprentice pilot. Good old Russ Jacobus in the engine room had a complete engineering crew with him.

Soon, at Lewes, Delaware, we dropped the pilots off on the pilot launch, and they were delivered to the pilot ship *Philadelphia*. Laying off the pilot puts the piloting responsibility on the captain, and he was soon busy with charts, laying courses and making estimates of ranges and times. Finally we passed Five Fathom Bank, and we were at sea.

Everyone was busy, some with oiler responsibilities in the engine room, some with deck watch, and still others in the galley, seeing that everyone was fed quite properly. We certainly did have unusual stores for a small ship passage; for instance, we had dozens of Chef Pierre pies baked and frozen in Traverse City, and we had trout, venison, and buffalo.

A deck watch consisted of three men, one on the wheel, one on lookout, and the other for miscellaneous duties such as getting coffee for the other two, or perhaps monitoring the radio or radar. Everything went well until the captain got a sun fix and found out that we were making only seven point nine knots. He was very unhappy, as was everyone else. After a board of directors meeting the Captain instructed "change engines," and soon the speed was in excess of ten knots.

Then, after a while the fog horn began to blow, and mass confusion set it—it was a fire drill. Everyone had their life jackets on their bunks, under their pillows and so a traffic jam set in. Finally, all had their life jackets on, or partially so, and were squirting water over the side until there were four streams of water going. They were all very proud until the captain announced that it took seven minutes, and it should have been done in less than two. The captain followed the fire drill with a long blast and three short blasts. What did that mean? We soon found out—an "abandon ship" drill. We learned by doing, as the captain was forming a real crew.

After some sunbathing the crew had to put on shirts. They were getting sunburned. This stretch between Cape May and Nantucket has a bad reputation, but the day we were on it, it was like Grand Traverse Bay in August.

During this wonderful day we saw perhaps fifty ships after leaving the shore, several large schools of blue whales, and porpoises, a number of Russian fishing trawlers, and a beautiful phosphorescence in the seas after dark—all of this in March.

The time is 10:00 P.M. the next day on the ship. The bridge watch consists of Bo Bosardet, Dr. Cline, with Paul Jones on the wheel. Everybody is straining his eyes to catch the first glimpse of the Nantucket Light, which will be the first marker we have sighted in some twenty-nine hours of flying blind, except for star and sun fixes. Everyone strains, the captain is on the bridge. Several off-duty crew members aid in the sea-

search. Then Warren Cline sings out, "I see it!" A twin flash. Soon we all see it, right on the nose, right in front of us. Nantucket Light.

If we had wanted more exciting seas, we soon got them. As we headed for Matinicus Light, near Penobscot Bay, the wind began to freshen and the skies turned gray. We couldn't go into Penobscot Bay without a pilot; the rocks would have finished us, so we shuttled back and forth in front of the light all night. Finally, after dawn, we headed for Castine and the Maine Maritime Academy.

Lieutenant Burris had warned about the Atlantic in winter; and it wasn't long before we understood what he meant. As we steamed along the coast of Nova Scotia, snow began to fall, and the sea was like a roller coaster. The washing machine had not been properly lashed, and it clattered across the floor. Cups, saucers, pots, and pans jumped around. It wasn't very easy to sleep that night.

Finally, however, the mouth of the St. Lawrence stretched before us, with ice floes in it the size of boats. We docked at Quebec, and the boat froze in while we slept. The next morning the propellers had to be used to break up the ice.

What we had decided was that we would like to be number one through the St. Lawrence Seaway in 1969. We were willing to wait six or seven days at Montreal to get that big permit; a second crew shipped on and before long we heard the news: we would be the first to lead the line through the locks.

We never used that permit. As we were getting ready to go, we saw a ship coming downriver with an eight-foot hole in its side. We decided to go second. "Let somebody else break the ice," Mike Hemmick said.

The new crew members, people like Al Balfour, insurance man Dick Mavis, racing-cruising expert Bud Sweeney, and surgeon Frank Power, encountered the worst fog some of them had ever seen right off Prescott, Ontario. Three times we had to drop anchor to wait for the fog to lift. We watched enormous ice floes, two to four feet thick and as big as ships bear down on us now.

In the sponge ice of Lake Erie the engines clogged; then we backflushed them and proceeded on to Detroit. TV cameramen swarmed on board again.

Meanwhile, the hometown was preparing a welcome. If I may be permitted, I'd like to quote from a newspaper article, this time from the *Detroit Free Press*, Sunday, April 20, 1969.

> This resort city of 18,432 at the foot of Grand Traverse Bay, which built itself a college a few years back, now proudly points to "our ship" the former *USS Allegheny.*
>
> Like the college, the ship materialized through local foresight, money and muscle. Both were the brain-children of Les Biederman, chief of the Paul Bunyan radio-television network.
>
> A volunteer crew of doctors, lawyers, professors and local merchants sailed the 142 foot diesel-electric Navy tug 3,500 miles from Philadelphia to Traverse City, ending the 29 day journey on schedule last week.
>
> Hundreds have crowded her decks on inspection tours since her arrival . . . "I was better off with a volunteer crew as far as getting work out of them" [Captain Hemmick said].

It had been a great twenty-nine days, a trip I would never forget, even as the maritime academy grew, eventually having as its commander retired admiral Willard Smith and graduating hundreds of successful merchant sailors. Not as the Allegheny served as a successful training ship and acquired a sister ship the *Hudson*, and especially not even when the old tug, and special ship, *Allegheny* sank in winter waters.

It had had a special kind of significance. It was a symbol more than a training ship, eventually. Nobody believed we could get a ship from the Navy, but thanks especially to Jerry Ford, we did. He had influence at the Defense Department, and I know it was Jerry that really swung the deal, and Bob Griffin pushed him into it. When that volunteer crew brought that ship to Traverse City, it was on the NBC news shows; it was on TV in Philadelphia and Detroit. It was kind of a triumphal tour, bringing that ship to Traverse City. The interesting thing is that at that particular time we had done a pretty good job to get the Legislature with us; we had a simple resolution, to get a maritime academy for the state and to establish it in Traverse City at Northwestern Michigan College. There was a lot of discouragement along the way, and of course a lot of other schools had said they wanted to have the school once it was announced. There was a great deal of conflict in setting it up. But when the Legislature voted on this, the Senate voted unanimously; Jack Toepp saw to that. When the House voted, there was only one dissenting vote, that was a member of the Maritime Union who was in the House at that time. The only reason we got this all done, and it had such a strong vote, was the pressure of the *Allegheny.* When that boat arrived in Detroit, a number of the legislators saw the ship and they couldn't believe it. "What a great thing this is for Michigan," they said, and then they voted on it.

The *Allegheny* sat in the harbor for ten years, being used for orientation and training courses; then, finally it had outlived its usefulness. The Board authorized me to sell it for $100,000. It was now our ship. If you have a surplus ship for ten years, you can do as you please with it. About this time, I got caught in a terrible storm while I was in the Marquette; and believe it or not, so much ice was formed on the side of the ship that the ship rolled over right on its side. Subsequently, would you believe that we sold that ship for $114,000, rolled over on its side like that? We got $14,000 more than we had expected to before it rolled over. The *Allegheny* was a very good thing. It was a symbol, it was the rallying point, it was the center of the issue. And, it worked. Because of it, we have the maritime academy today. Without it, I don't think we would have the maritime academy.

* * * * *

Traverse City had begun to grow at a phenomenal rate. The entire area was exploding, and I began to talk on the radio a lot about the growth and what that would mean to the area. I predicted that Traverse would become the hub of a great area of 100,000, serving as a service community center for all the other areas. Industry of a certain sort would continue, the resort trade would grow and prosper, but mostly Traverse City would benefit from having people come up and settle, retire or relocate in this beautiful area which had so many plusses. They would create jobs, service occupations and professions for each other; and we all needed to be prepared for a great surge of continuing growth, construction and change in the area.

The editorials continued; here are sample ones from the 1970's. One thing that is obvious is that I could change my mind; note the editorial on the power plant.

Monday, October 13, 1970

THE LOCAL POWER PLANT

For a long time some local residents have been opposed to the City owning its own power plant, particularly since the large green addition on the Bay, and even more particularly since cocktail conversation hinges on air and water pollution.

Within the next two or three years, it is very likely that we in our City will count our blessings as a result of the construction of the power plant, and particularly since the recent addition. This comes from your editor who felt that the addition was much too big for our needs. You see, the power plant that was in place before the addition sits there complete, unused except for emergency; and the big new addition in supplying the City with its power needs runs much below capacity.

The power load in Traverse City could increase greatly with the shortage of electricity, and this is no doubt going to happen. The great debt that the City has contracted to pay off the additions may turn out to be a great idea, and all of this for several unrelated reasons.

First, the public utilities such as Consumers Power are in a real bind. The ecologists are on their back, and they are having much trouble and will have more in locating power plants. Most of the problems we think are ficticious, such as heating of the water in Lake Michigan, but the problem is there, and precious time is being lost in construction and operation of major plants to supply the needs of the State of Michigan. This same thing holds true in the surrounding area, where cooperating programs permit an interchange of electric power. Therefore, it could be that in Traverse City and the area served by the locally owned power plant, there will be no power shortage, whereas in the other parts of the state there could be real problems. This is not because the public utilities are not aware of the problem, and not because they aren't willing to provide the services; but the ecologists are on their back, and the cost of constructing power plants is still increasing at a great rate.

It takes about five years to get a major power plant in operation from the planning stage, but the public each day finds more use for that precious voltage that they have found so reliable in the past. With the time factor and the opposition and the cost of money and the cost of construction, the public utilities are in a real bind.

But take a look at our local municipal power plant. There it sits, with some 15,000 kilowatts of generating capacity sitting idle, both boilers and generators, and yet still having capacity in the new addition.

The local situation is solid for still another reason. In case of break down, the generating facilities of the REA's are interconnected with the plant, and they could come to the aid of the city if necessary. We have aided them with millions of kilowatts of interchange, and that should work in reverse in case of problems.

Therefore, within the next five years, it could be that our economic picture will improve because all of this power plant construction took place and the necessary kilowatts for new industry or new home use are available, whereas the public utilities may have problems in meeting their needs for their present customers in other parts of the State.

Friday, October 30, 1970

OUR CATHOLIC FRIENDS WORK VERY HARD AT SUPPORTING THEIR OWN SCHOOLS

It has been our experience to have worked very hard to get votes for operating millage and capital millage for our public schools.

We have been pleased to have Catholic friends also working diligently on the same campaigns, even though their children were attending parochial schools.

The members of the Catholic Church have, in addition to paying the taxes for the support of the public schools, supported their own schools and at a tremendous sacrifice. For instance, recently even though most of the families make regular contributions and tuition payments for the support of St. Francis School, there was a serious deficit. Some 750 families made additional pledges amounting to nearly a quarter of a million dollars over a two-year period to pay off the deficit in the operations.

We well remember the campaign to construct the St. Francis Gym and the St. Francis High School. The families really dug deep to provide these facilities. In the support of many of the perimeter activities at St. Francis, they use more gimmicks and public participation than most would believe. Every child that attends these parochial schools is a reduction in the tax burden of the local electorate.

As a result of our editorial of yesterday, many people interpreted that we indicated that our opinion was to vote "yes," which is in effect killing Parochaid. We intended no such endorsement, nor did we endorse the other side.

We have not, nor are we now taking sides on the issue as to whether or not one should vote for or against the Constitutional amendment. We are merely setting the record straight about the job that these good people have done up to now to provide for what they think is important.

We do not believe that our function is to bend the voter one way or the other, but we do believe that we may help in setting the record straight, and in this editorial we are reminding the entire electorate of the money sacrifices that our Catholic Brothers not only made but are continuing to make day by day and far into the future.

Thursday, July 1, 1971

BOY, DID I EVER FIND OUT WHAT A SQUARE I WAS

Last evening, a town meeting was held in the Park Place Motor Inn Dome. It was called by the Council on Drug and Alcohol

Abuse. It was chaired by the County Welfare Director, and first off, we take our hat off to him for a job well done.

All types of people were there, street people, establishment people, medical people, and others. It was quite an assembly. Many bitter words were said, but many helpful and friendly words also. There was much interest in this problem, not only from the proponents of the use of dope (and they were legion), but much interest on the part of what we might call establishment people.

We think that this meeting of the minds and the sharing of opinions changed few minds, but did make much thinking take place. We think such meetings are needed, and it was as good as we have ever attended.

Now, about my being so square. I always thought grass was the stuff that wouldn't grow on the lawn and then grew too much and required a lot of care. We thought grass was the mother of dandelions.

We thought pigs were raised by farmers to provide us with pork. We thought that law enforcement officers were policemen. We found out that people all over the place were getting busted, and it finally sunk in, they were being arrested.

We think that for a starter, we should confer respect on others that we expect for ourselves. For instance, how can a person with an unshaven face, and long hair, in bare feet, call a policeman that is hired by us, the public, a pig and expect to get respectful treatment in return.

Many of those, for the most part young people but not all, goad the police at night. We see it in the evening when we come down town to write the editorial for the following day. Our parking lot some nights seem like an expressway. With or without long hair, let us treat people as people, with due respect, and let us also demand such respect in return. This will aid in the solution of what we are calling a problem.

Tuesday, July 20, 1971

A WELL-KNOWN AMERICAN COMPANY LABEL ON A TV SET DOES MEAN IT WAS MADE IN AMERICA

The latest country coming up fast in manufacturing consumer products for sale in these United States is Taiwan. Big things are happening there. Every man hour of work performed in places such as Taiwan could be performed by the many unemployed in America. We pay unemployment and relief funds to American unemployed and tax the American people to provide these funds. If the lost man hours in this country were equated with the relief costs, we are sure that American products would cost less than the foreign imports.

Taiwan is emerging as a TV superpower. Taiwan expects monthly TV exports in 1972 to reach 200,000 per month. This is roughly two and a half million per year. These will carry famous American corporation labels, such as Sylvania, Zenith, Admiral, Philco-Ford and RCA.

The same thing is happening in Mexico, but to a smaller extent. We have pointed out many times that consumer radios are not made at all in our country. They are all imported. And now it is happening in TV.

This process of using cheap foreign labor is now big time, and we are seeing the small ticket radio being superceded by the big ticket television set.

Millions of American consumers will be purchasing expensive color receivers in the next few years, and we ask, "Who will build them?" We think it would be sensible for us to seriously evaluate the unemployment cost in this country versus the cost of the foreign-made receiver and see how we come out.

We don't know of a single study to determine this cost. But we do have studies about the sex life of grasshoppers in ancient Greece.

Soon, we will have smiling foreign faces doing all of our work. This sounds great, but we will all be unemployed with no money to buy—then what?

This not only holds true with radio and television, but with many other items such as cars, raw steel, aluminum and other items. Our big problem is to get Americans gainfully employed, not the people of Taiwan, and other such distant places.

Monday, July 26, 1971

CONGRATULATIONS ROY AND ELLEN BRIGMAN

Today starts the twentieth encampment of Camp Roy-El. For those of our listeners that are not informed about this, let us give you a thumbnail sketch.

Twenty years ago, a young married couple in this city, dedicated to aiding handicapped children, started a summer camp for these youngsters. They have been able to develop a real team of volunteer workers to aid in this endeavor. One of the brightest things about it are the teenaiders. This is a large group of teenage youngsters who work without pay to help the handicapped in this week-long encampment. They operate no financial campaign, but get lots of help, given freely by citizens who think of others rather than themselves.

The first year of this program saw fifteen handicampers, fourteen teenaiders, and six staff members. This year, there will be between 100 and 110 handicampers, 50 teenaiders, and a large staff.

This encampment is held at Gilbert Lodge, the 4-H camping facility, the real estate of which has been given to the program by the late Judge Parm Gilbert. Many of the facilities at the 4-H camp were provided by a man and woman that we are proud to know, Jerry and Frances Oleson, who have contributed much to make this the success that it is.

This encampment will last for two weeks, starting today, and we know that some of our summer visitors will be interested in this program. They are encouraged to visit it during the next two weeks at Gilbert Lodge, the 4-H camp.

We would be remiss if we didn't express our appreciation to all of the people who work at this venture, particularly the teenage teenaiders. You hear about the drug cult, the rebellious youngsters, but how about our teenaiders? Do they not deserve as much publicity as a demonstration of protest? These young people are doing a real service to handicapped youngsters. And we pay tribute to the adults that help with the program. Without them, it just wouldn't work. And to Roy and Ellen, again we say a simple "thanks" for the dedication during these twenty years and the fine results that have been achieved.

Friday, July 30, 1971

THE PROSPECTORS CLUB

We have many fine service clubs in Traverse City, and several in the smaller cities surrounding us. One of the most unusual is a county service club, if you would call it that. It is the Prospectors Club, and it consists of representatives from all over the county, with a couple of representatives from the neighboring town of Traverse City.

Last evening the Prospectors Club met at the Leland Lodge, and it sure was different from my last visit. Al Wrisley has completely refurbished it, added to it and brought it right up to date, yet it still has the charm of the former years. By the way, Al Wrisley is the direct descendant of one of the first settlers in this region, who settled at Northport.

The Prospectors Club is an interesting one. It brings all walks of life together. For instance, this year the President is a farmer, Glen Noonan. The Secretary is Everett Delong, who for many years held office in the Court House.

Among the members of the Club is Fred Roth, some eighty years of age, who was born in Leland, and has lived his entire life in and around that community. Just think, Fred was born at that site, some thirty years after the first White Man settled there.

Among the members are a number of interesting people, among them Jim Carlson, the senior fisherman from Fishtown, who has spent his entire life pursuing his trade as fisherman, as did his father before him, and probably his grandfather.

Talking to these old-timers about when they were youngsters is exciting. How many of you knowledgeable people, for instance, know that Leland was the site of not only a wooding station for the steamers, but also of an iron plant that made wrought iron before steel was so commonplace? This is the kind of iron the blacksmiths worked with. They brought the ore in by boat, and the site of the works was the present site of the marina. They used charcoal made from hardwood in the forest, and the charcoal kilns were at the present site of the Bluebird Restaurant. Much valuable history is passing and not being recorded. We just wish that all of our listeners could have shared this visit with the Prospectors Club.

Note: Shortly after this editorial, I suggested to the people at Pathfinder School, who were then in the process of founding the school, that there was a real need for some group to put on tape the memories of these old-timers. As a result of that conversation, they set up the Pioneer Study Center, which has taped over 100 of these memories and which is publishing this book.

CHAPTER EIGHT

EIGHTIES AND NINETIES

And so now the century is in its eighties and I am in my seventies. I have a lot to look back on, and a lot to look forward to, as anyone does who has reasonably good health and a variety of interests. There have been logical changes in the Paul Bunyan network; the cablevision network merged in August of 1982 with the Centel Corporation, which is the fourth largest telephone company in the United States. In the last couple of years we have increased our power in the Traverse City station. In order to do that, we have had to sell three of the stations—Cadillac, Petoskey and Gaylord, because you can't have two radio stations covering the same market. In 1980 we merged the television station with U.S. Tobacco Company of Greenwich, Connecticut. It was going to take about a million dollars to bring that station up to date, and we didn't have the million. U.S. Tobacco has put a million dollars into the operation, and they are running an excellent TV station.

As I look at my situation now, I see that one of the things I have to be grateful for is that I have always had excellent people to work with in radio. Surely some of the most outstanding of these were right at WTCM in Traverse City. I have mentioned my working partners, but there are others. Ken Haven came to us in 1945, and he has been an absolutely outstanding newsman and radio personality. Intelligent, thorough, and always professional, Ken has been one of the real assets to the station through the years. Leon Bush also came to us after the war and was a significant force at the station; he is now working with the TV operation. Ralph Diethelm of Alpena and Gordon Brogden of our sales department have been standouts, as I think of my past associations at the station; and I'm always amazed at the enthusiasm of the young kids who keep coming to us to keep the station lively and up-to-date.

One of my deepest concerns in the past few years, both on the air and personally, has been the subject of energy. My first interest in this subject began when I was about nine and was riding on the Lizzie boat down the Delaware River. I looked down in the hold and saw that black man shovelling coal into the boiler and then looked down the next door, which had been opened for ventilation, and saw those wonderful engines. My interest in energy was re-awakened when I went to Cooke Junior High and spent a good deal of time in the engine room with Mr. Pritchard, the school's engineer. Here steam engines were running, generating electricity.

Even at that age my mind was running on, projecting. I wondered why you couldn't take the electricity that was coming out of those engines, put a bunch of hot plates in the boiler, and let them boil the water and run the engine instead of having to use coal. Mr. Pritchard sat down and laboriously explained to me about the efficiency of combustion. He said there was no such thing as perpetual motion, and that loss of energy would eventually cause the engines to slow down and stop.

I became fascinated with the idea that some engines are more efficient than others, and I studied the Corliss engine to see why it was more efficient than the Ames. It used less steam, it seemed, and therefore required less coal. This interest in energy has been lifelong, and when the power plant was built in Traverse City, I was a frequent visitor. I liked to watch the old steam pumps and steam turbines. Through all these experiences, I learned quite a bit about electric power generation.

In 1973 the world experienced the Arab oil embargo. Prior to that time power plants were converting from coal to oil, because oil was easier to use than coal and didn't require the man power to operate and supervise its processes. After the Arab oil embargo arrived, this country had the hands of monopoly around its throat, with OPEC controlling the world oil supply. What could the world do about assuring a consistent energy supply in the future?

I spent a lot of time thinking about the problem of energy supply. What substitute could we have for oil? Coal wasn't a total answer; coal mining is difficult, and we kill 100 miners a year in mine accidents. In addition coal causes pollution problems.

I thought of the other options being discussed by experts, and they all seemed to have disadvantages. After awhile, and quite naturally, I began to consider wood as an excellent energy answer for the country; and wood became another cause for me to take up.

I began to visit schools of forestry, such as Cornell, Michigan State and the University of Michigan, and I learned many, many things about wood and forestry. What I learned convinced me that wood has a real future use for energy purposes, and I don't know why more is not actively being done to promote its use in that way.

First of all, wood is a non-polluting energy agent. It does not have the sulpher in it that other agents do, and so when it burns it does not pollute the air. What's more, wood is easy to get—forever ready for us out in our countryside. This is particularly true today, as wood is being managed as a crop in forest industries. In my research I discovered that forests today actually provide two crops, and these two over and over again. The first crop, big trees, can provide enormous amounts of wood if the trees are allowed to grow to maximum size. This will happen if the underbrush is thinned and controlled so that it does not deprive the larger trees of moisture and room. The small trees, in addition, can be themselves used and thus become the second crop.

I learned how the process of forest cropping is actually done in 1977 when I met Norval Morey, the president and principal owner of Morbark Industries in Winn, Michigan, a small town near Mt. Pleasant. Norval Morey has made a lifework out of manufacturing forest-cropping equipment. He built de-barkers and then chippers, and then turned his efforts towards developing a shear which eliminated the need for chainsaws. Instead of sawing a tree. The woodsman can clip it in two with a device that is mounted on the front of a tractor, and resembles a pair of giant scissors. Nub Morrey also developed machines to haul wood out to the chippers and de-barkers. All of these machines serve the important purpose of mechanizing the forest industries.

Nub showed me that you can go into a forest and crop thirty to fifty tons of undergrowth per acre and utilize that, at the same time freeing larger trees to grow twice as fast. Thus the forest will become more productive for marketable timber.

But just marketable timber? I began to get excited as I thought of the possibilities of this wood for use in generating energy. How about using woodchips made in these machines for power generation? I discovered that one ton of wood chips cut out of the forest in the way I have described is equivalent to one and seven-tenths barrels of oil. A ton of wood chips costs about fifteen or twenty dollars, while the heating equivalency of a barrel of oil costs about sixty dollars, so there is a real economic advantage in wood. Of course, as is obvious, it will take an awful lot of wood chips to produce enough fuel to generate significant amounts of electricity. In fact, if you were to fuel a 10,000 watt power plant, which would really be the smallest feasible power plant you could build, you would need 100,000 tons of chips a year to provide fuel.

Where would you get this 100,000 tons a year? What you really need is about 20,000 acres of forest nearby. That really isn't a very big circle of forests, but with different people owning the land, you could run into some serious problems in acquiring enough wood. Another problem is that you can haul only twenty tons in a load, which for the plant I'm thinking of would involve 5,000 truckloads, an awfully expensive hauling situation.

It wasn't until I went down the Inland Waterway recently that I saw how these problems involving wood for energy production could be solved. Along the waterway were two resources together: a great deal of barge traffic and hundreds of miles of seemingly unmanaged forests. Using these two resources, the barge traffic and the forests, a company would have an opportunity to thin forests for hundreds of miles, and with a little planning, to set up power plants which would use wood as fuel in an efficient manner with a good distribution system.

Here is how it could be done. Companies could set up barges complete with chippers, and they could cut and load wood onto these barges for one tenth the cost of hauling it by truck. Small floating power plants could even be mounted on barges. These boat-plants could probably be mass produced in a shipyard for far less money than it would take to build power plants on land. They would operate with water coming in one end of the barges and going out the other end, thus cooling the turbines. Also, during construction, heavy equipment such as turbines, could be hauled on barges to the boat-plants at their sites, thus saving money on shipping costs.

You know, nobody has ever constructed a thing like a floating power plant, and I just keep looking at the idea and wondering. Wood is an amazingly renewable resource. For instance, if a company was to use the forests along the waterways I saw, they could slowly thin for ten years and then go back to where they had begun, because the undergrowth would be grown up there again. They could crop a ten-mile wide stretch of forest and operate a power plant with wood forever this way. It isn't happening there as of now, of course. The power plants I saw along the way were diesel plants or steam plants with oil-fired boilers. A wood-fired plant along a waterway would save a tremendous amount of that oil and make our nation more energy independent than it now is.

And the Inland waterway is only one of many American waterways lined with timber. The New York Barge Canal alone has a fifty-mile stretch of swampy, heavily-timbered land. Some land on Long Island, which has such tremendous energy needs, also has heavy wood resources. Think of the Mississippi River! The tree growth along that waterway is very rapid, because the climate is warm and there is a lot of water available. Wood-fueled power plants of the type I have described would work very well on the Mississippi. Once the wood chips were cut along any of these waterways, they could be delivered at a reasonable cost by tugboats pulling 3,000 tons of chips as far as two hundred miles in one day. Think what that would save in trucking fees. No money towards licenses, tires, insurance, depreciation! A tug-waterway system would be less expensive.

The way I see it, the energy generated by wood could be distributed through a new tier of service companies that would generate electricity for wholesale use only at low cost. These would supplement our present public-owned utilities and provide an extra energy source in an efficient way.

The forests, of course, near to the floating power plants I am envisioning, would have to be managed forests. What I am talking about is the energy plantation. Right now, by and large, we raise our wood supply by letting God plant it, take care of it, and mature it, for whatever harvest there will be. This random approach has real problems if you care about yield. Trees cease to grow when light supply drops down to a certain level. Undergrowth, as we have said, competes with trees and slows their growth patterns. Food and water come when they want to.

I wonder what would happen if we cultivated corn in the same way we "cultivate" our forests? If we let God plant our corn, germinate it and take care of it, we wouldn't have much corn would we? Now, we have to carefully plant it, fertilize it, till it. We develop selective seed, each year a little better. Why don't we do all these things with our forests? We could increase our wood yield four or fivefold. The Weyerhauser Company is now selling lumber from trees that are only forty years old. If they had used Nature's method, it would have taken them 120 years to produce equivalent size trees.

On the energy plantation, scientists would improve trees through careful genetic selection. Small trees would be kept for a significant period inside, where they would grow twenty-four hours a day, 365 days a year. We would not settle for trees which grow as Nature does it, only fifty percent of the time. We would produce super trees as a crop, and with such plantations, we would eliminate some of our dependency on oil for generating electricity.

I haven't even mentioned the use of wood for home heating, which is obviously increasing, or the use of wood to produce alcohol to replace the alcohol now produced by grain. I think we are on the threshold of something very exciting, as we use wood for energy and make one of Nature's great gifts a resource for the planet's future.

* * * *

Energy is not the only subject I am considering as I let my mind venture into the future at this point in my life. The college I've loved is a very important thing in my thinking, and I'm often writing a little essay in my mind, entitled "Whither Northwestern Michigan College?" I have an idea for the college, and as I told Con Foster in that letter so many years ago, I'm not trying to tell anybody what to do, just pointing out what *might* happen if anyone is in the mood for a little visionary future-building.

Here is the idea. Now, Northwestern Michigan was started in an unusual way. It was, and is, a people's college. Since it is different from other colleges, it seems to me it should build on its sense of difference by continuing to take bold, new tacks that will bring it, in the space of only a few years, to the status of a university.

This can be done without the gigantic expenditure of major funds to add two full years of programs to the curriculum. Instead, NMC could become an association of colleges, a university of satellite institutions of learning. In Traverse City, grouped around the central campus, could be a religious college, a technological institute and other specialized colleges, some of them four-year schools. Thus, we would be a university, like universities in the Middle Ages and like colleges such as Cambridge in England today. It seems, of course, overwhelming to think about starting other four-year colleges, but if NMC's resources, already available and functioning, were utilized, would-be schools could be helped on their way to opening.

Here is a scenario detailing what I'm talking about. Suppose you are a group which wishes to establish a college in Michigan. There are many educational specifications you must meet, and that can be done, but there is one hard-core specification you must meet that is very difficult for most groups—you must have a million dollars worth of assets. With my concept, that could be overcome with only half the work. (I've discussed this idea with the graduate school people in education at Michigan State and University of Michigan, and they agree this will work.) Your group enters into an agreement with Northwestern Michigan College, which is authorized to do all kinds of basic college course work, even beyond the first two years of college, to provide two years of the basic work towards the degree. Then, according to interpretation of the present state law, your group would be responsible for only half a million capitalization, because Northwestern Michigan's facilities and coursework would represent the other half.

Your group would use our library, our eating facilities, our dorms and special services. Your group would provide the special educational program you wish for the final two years.

Through utilizing the facilities already available at our college, your job would be cut in half. You wouldn't have to stop at raising half a million, though. I believe it is possible to raise another half a million, possibly more, to start up the proper kind of satellite college here; for instance, a petroleum institute. If we assisted a new school and you had one million to work with, half of that could go towards building new facilities for your school. The other half could be set up as an endowment fund, to provide fifty thousand dollars a year, coming in to underwrite your program and supplement your tuition and donation program. Northwestern Michigan could set aside a small piece of land for your new school. You would need a faculty of only four or five, at least in the beginning. There you are with everything but your school colors chosen for you!

A petroleum institute is a real natural for this area, and I think there is definite support for it. But what about a religious school? It is not very difficult to start a religious college in Michigan, and with the incentives I've suggested, there must be several church groups who might be interested. Why not make a survey of all the religious organizations, particularly the Catholic Church, which has, I believe, thirty-seven or thirty-eight organizations operating colleges, to see which ones want to have a school in Michigan. Then negotiate a deal. Now, when you have got three or four of these colleges, what do you have? You have a university.

There is such a college in Fairmount, California. Pomona College was the nucleus of such a university. It had begun in Pomona, but during the depression they found an unusual way to grow. They discovered a large building in Fairmount which was not being completed because of lack of funds, so they bought this unfinished structure and moved their college to Fairmount. When the building was finished, a group of people wanted to start another type of college; and Fairmount College was set up near the same site. Then, someone wanted a college for women there, so the Scripps family underwrote the founding of Scripps College for Women. These three colleges banded together and created another unit called the

Associated Graduate School. The presidency of Associated Graduate School is rotated among the heads of the three schools there. I don't know any reason why this can't be used as a pattern for Northwestern Michigan, which is going to have to grow in some new way and may as well move in a creative, innovative direction. Well, like all the rest of these things that have come to me since I've moved to Traverse City, it is only an idea.

* * * *

One of the best things about being a little older is that you don't have to feel guilty about taking time for hobbies you've always loved but couldn't afford the time and money to pursue. I've always loved boats, from the earliest days in Philadelphia on, and it's obvious that this is going to be a real interest for me as the future unfolds.

In the 1950's I bought an old wreck in Leland. The *Helen S* had been an old fishing tug, but it was now rotted, truly in sad shape. I had it loaded on a trailer and brought to my backyard while my wife was in Philadelphia. It sat on blocks in the backyard for four years while I restored it. Eventually it became a fine little yacht, which I christened the *Ho-Maid.*

The *Ho-Maid* accompanied forty-seven consecutive yacht races during a ten-year period. I relayed radio reports on races to Northport, Manitou Island, and other ports of call where Grand Traverse region sailors were competing for yacht club trophies. I remember one in particular—a Beaver Island race in 1969. It was a foggy weekend on the Great Lakes and I had gone ahead of the fleet about ten or fifteen miles; I was on the only one of all the Traverse City boats which had a radio, as we headed up the main channel towards Mackinac. Suddenly it seemed as if we were surrounded by steamers, which shouldn't have been too unusual, seeing as how we were in the steamer track.

There were seven or eight boats behind me, and that fog

was dense. It seemed to me the steamers might not be aware of our little sailboats from Traverse, so I radioed, "There are six or eight racing sailboats right in the steamer track, so be extra careful."

The steamers radioed back, "We have our radar on, and we don't see any sailboats."

I asked them what range they had, and they replied eighteen miles. "Put it on six miles and you'll see something you'd better avoid!" I said. They did and still couldn't see anything.

"Put it on a half mile!" I shouted into the radio and almost instantly I could hear the sounds of five loud blasts, as the ships put their engines on strong reverse to avoid the boats right in front of them. Our fleet was becalmed in the fog; and these huge steamers came to a stop, dead in the water, to avoid overrunning them. I was pretty glad for my training as a radio operator then.

My sons grew up, and they weren't very interested in doing the maintenance on the boat. It was wooden and the maintenance requirements were pretty stiff; I was involved with the cable TV business. The *Ho-Maid* sat in back of the station for six or seven years, slowly going to pot, until a young man in Traverse fell in love with it; and since he was willing to take good care of it and repair it, I gave it to him.

I still wanted a boat, and I began to look around. I didn't want any boat; I wanted something special. There were so many people that had meant something to me, relatives, associates in the radio business, Traverse City people—I wanted to be able to take them on boat rides they would never forget, just as I was taken for boat rides when I was a child. There had been quite a few projects for the city; this one would be for me. I would get something I could cruise the inland waterways with, to satisfy my life-long fascination with these wonderful water highways in the United States. I had avidly read about the Erie Canal, dug by hand through New York in the 1830's, part of which eventually became the commercial New York Barge Canal. I wanted to travel that, and also the inland waterways from the Delaware River all the way to Florida, past historic spots that George Washington had surveyed, past water birds and tidal basins. I wanted to see it all.

I asked to see some boats for sale. The plans came for a certain fifty-three foot boat, and I showed them to Anne. This boat had nice accommodations on the first level, but the eating and galley space was on the lower level. She pointed out that some of our friends were getting older, and it would be difficult for them to scramble down all those stairs. So we looked at a fifty-eight foot boat. Same situation; below stairs accommodations. Then the broker sent me plans for a boat that was out of this world, but I thought it was also out of my league; too expensive for a boy from Fishtown, even though he was now quite comfortably provided for.

After many phone calls, I decided to take a look at the boat in Ft. Lauderdale, and when I got there, lo and behold, there it was, the boat of my dreams, my *Happy Days.* I've got to say that I didn't realize how big it was, really. When Ken Thompson and I got to Ft. Lauderdale, the boat was moored in a shipyard in a building with a large roof. There was a boat alongside of it that was 120 feet long, on the other side there was a Burger yacht that was ninety feet long; and here in between them was this little sixty-two footer. It didn't look very big to me. We climbed all over it, and it was beautiful. It had a nice dining room and full kitchen on the main level, a lovely main salon, and plenty of cabins for visiting NBC executives or cousins from Philadelphia, if I should want to invite them aboard.

We went to dicker with the broker and decided to make a deal. By noon we were all finished. As Ken and I were having lunch, talking over our purchase, some men near us said, "So you guys are buying the Abscam boat." We looked at them, bewildered.

We went back to the broker and asked about the boat's history. He thought we already knew about it, but since we didn't, he filled us in. Walter Rex, of Walter Rex Maritime Imports in Ft. Lauderdale, had had the boat built in Hong Kong; and it had become his personal yacht. He had then sold it to the president of Venezuela, who sold it to two mysterious people who left it adrift in the Gulf Stream, with six million dollars worth of marijuana stowed in its cabins. It was publicized as the million dollar yacht found adrift.

The Coast Guard confiscated the boat, and when the FBI was looking for a boat for the Abscam caper, they set up cameras on the boat and used it for the notorius payoffs involving congressmen. Later the original owner saw it come up on the bid list of the boatyard and bought it, reconditioned it, and sold it to us. Quite a history.

I left Ft. Lauderdale with a commercial captain, the first of three. When Anne and I reached New Smyrna, we had a massive electrical short circuit, and we had to re-wire the boat. My grandson Greg and I, and a captain then proceeded to Hilton Head (Anne had decided to return to take care of the house for a while; she rejoined us in Philly). Now this captain had run the boat aground a couple of times, and by this time I had about convinced myself that I could navigate and operate this boat as well as that captain. Besides, I was paying this guy $100 a day to do what I had bought the boat to do myself. So, from Hilton Head on up my grandson Greg and I took that boat up to Philadelphia. We had a glorious time from then on in. We went to Washington, D.C., where we had people from the legal profession, congressmen and others I knew come on board; but it was in Philly that I had the most fun.

In Philadelphia people I hadn't seen in a long time came down. We had intended to stay a week; instead we stayed three weeks so we could visit all our relatives and friends from the old days. One night I wandered down and looked around on the Delaware River. I saw an old ship, a tug, and began to nose around. The captain came out, an older man, and asked what I was up to. I told him that this tug reminded me of the Lizzie and Johnny boats I had ridden as a youth. He became excited and clapped me on the shoulder. "You rode the Lizzie and Johnny boats? I don't believe it." He called other captains and seamen in the area by radio and they came down and we had a real confab. It seems that there is a movement afoot now to find out more about the history of those boats and perhaps restore the rides in some way. I was the only "kid" they had ever found who had actually ridden on one of the boats, and I was a rare exhibit to them. We agreed to keep in touch.

While we were there, the Queen Elizabeth II came into Philadelphia, and we escorted her forty-five miles up the Delaware to her berth. Then wc had some cousins come aboard who were going to stay with us just till Cape May, New Jersey. We had such a good time they stayed aboard until we got to Traverse City and stayed a week with us here in Traverse.

So I got to cruise the Inland Waterway, and it was everything I had ever expected. There is no more beautiful way to see America, any part of it, than from a boat. And, because I believe this, I'm now at work on a new little project. I'm having benches built to put on the decks of the *Happy Days*, so I can take lots of kids out on Grand Traverse Bay. There are about five hundred of them going to go in August of '82 alone, and many of them have never been out on our beautiful Bay. I guess I won't be able to serve them any tomato soup, and maybe that'll be a little sad. Somehow a boat ride just doesn't seem like a boat ride to me without tomato soup and soda crackers.

The End